OUT OF DA NANG

A Lightning Source Book
Published by Lightning Source
1246 Heil Quaker Blvd.
La Vergne, TN USA 37086

Copyright 2012 by E.P. Moore
Book design by Dori Beeler
Cover design by Dori Beeler
Edited by Sandra Rea

For information regarding special discounts for bulk purchases, please contact Lightning Source at: inquiry@lightningsource.com
Phone: (615) 213-5815

ISBN: 978-0-615-64501-8

Every effort has been made to make this book as complete and as accurate as possible. However, there may be mistakes, both typographical and in content.

The purpose of this book is to educate and entertain. The stories are based on real-life events, though names have been for the most part changed to protect identities and privacy. The author and publisher shall have neither liability nor responsibility to any person or entity with respect to any loss or damage caused, or alleged to have been caused, directly or indirectly, by the information contained in this book.

If you do not wish to be bound by the above, you may return this book to the publisher for a full refund.

OUT

OF

DA NANG

DEDICATION

To my wife, Trish, who encouraged me and whom I love with all my
heart. Trish, you are my one and only, my real-life Rose Ann.

TABLE OF CONTENTS

ACKNOWLEDGMENTS

This novel, although fictional, originates and was sparked by true-life experiences. Names have been changed; some have remained true to character with permission. The stories are true in nature and have come from either my life or from real after-action reports long ago declassified.

There are multitudes of people I wish to thank. First and foremost, I give thanks to all servicemen… not just the Marine Corps, but to the men and women from all branches of the military that sacrificed so much for our great nation. Whether volunteers or called to duty, what they have done for our great nation can never be repaid.

I will always carry the title Marine; I earned it. I spent six years on active duty serving on both the east coast and west coast with one tour of duty in Viet Nam flying Sikorsky UH34D helicopters. I entered the Corps as a Private and was honorably discharged, having been selected for promotion to Captain. I know from personal experiences what sacrifices our young men and women have given to our great nation.

Those who challenge the United States of America should read our history, stand for one hour and look out over one of our national cemeteries. They're filled with men and women of all colors, all races, and all religions… men and women who were united in the cause and protection of freedom. To they who are now at rest and at peace, I dedicate this book.

PROLOGUE

As you enter Arlington National Cemetery
Arlington, Virginia, a sign reads:

Welcome to Arlington National Cemetery
Our Nations Most Sacred Shrine

Please Conduct Yourselves with Dignity
And Respect at All Times

Please remember these are Hallowed Grounds

Atop a rolling hill facing our nation's capital of Washington, D.C., a white marble sarcophagus stands in honor of those fallen in battle. It bears three Greek figures representing Peace, Victory, and Valor. Within the crypt lies a fallen hero from World War I. A profound inscription reads, "Here Rests in Honored Glory an American Soldier Known But to God." Adjacent to this sarcophagus lie the crypts of the unknowns from World War II, the Korean War, and the Viet Nam War.

On March 25, 1926, the Third Infantry Regiment U.S. Army was assigned the task of guarding the Tombs of the Unknown at Arlington National Cemetery during daylight hours. Better known to the public as the "Old Guard," an elite group of men have been selected internally from this unit over the years. These men have the honored duty of guarding the tombs and laying to rest our fallen heroes. Since July 2, 1937, 24 hours a day, 365 days a year, and regardless of weather, these soldiers never leave their post. They have dedicated their lives to our fallen heroes. On this day, February 26, 1966, in this most hallowed ground 1st Lt. Edward P. Blizzard, USMCR 085960, was laid to rest. **Peace, Granted Through Death.**

CHAPTER 1
ARLINGTON NATIONAL CEMETARY

Carried by wheeled caisson, Lt. Blizzard's casket, draped with our nation's flag, had just arrived at Section 70, Grave S-38, Grid EF-22. At the
site were four representatives of the Old Guard, eight Marine pallbearers,
a bugler, 10 rifle bearers, a beautiful young woman, and an abundance of
Lt. Blizzard's friends and fellow Marine officers. The woman appeared to
be a close friend of Lt. Blizzard's. Of the three men seated in the V.I.P. section, one was obviously an Apache representative, because he was in full
Indian Dress. The rest were made up of Lt. Blizzard's father, the young
woman, and a man in military uniform that I knew to be Lt. General Lewis
E. Walters. He was the Commanding General (MAAG) Military Assistance Group Viet Nam, the recipient of two Navy Crosses and a Silver
Star for Bravery. He was also the officer in charge (OIC) of the day's
proceedings.

As I approached the gravesite I could hear General Walters reading what
would be the final and last citation awarded to Lt. Blizzard. I could hear
muffled words though understanding little. Words like "heroic achievement, helicopter pilot, well armed, though wounded" drifted into the air.
After the reading of Lt. Blizzard's citation General Walters stepped back
from the the casket, saluted and marched past the Honor Guard to a posi-

tion on the left and to the foot of the casket. It was a somber moment.

At this point, the representative from the Apache Nation placed a blue stone on the casket and performed a eulogy that emphasized Lt. Blizzard's devotion to country, his Apache brothers, and the Corps. I was mesmerized by his words. "Apache brothers" rang in my ears. When finished, he stepped back and placed himself two steps behind the OIC. The bugler played taps, the formal folding of the flag was completed, and one of the pallbearers handed the flag to General Walters who then executed an about face, marched toward Lt. Blizzard's father and said in a voice that almost cracked, "This flag is presented on behalf of a grateful nation as a token of appreciation for the honorable and faithful service rendered by your son, 1st Lt. Edward Blizzard."

The father's only response was a simple, "Thank you." He stared at the flag blankly and only looked up when the General began to speak.

"Sir, it has been a honor to have served with and personally known a Marine such as your son. I owe him my life." The General stepped back adding, "This concludes the services at this time." At this point, the young woman sobbed as if inconsolable.

I approached General Walters and Lt. Blizzard's father, extending my hand first to Mr. Blizzard and then to the General. "My name is Bill Waterman," I said, addressing the fallen soldier's father. "I'm a writer for a number of newspapers in the Washington area and with your consent, Sir, I'd like to do a series of articles and a military chronicle about your son's duty to our country."

Both men stared into my eyes as if to be searching my soul for an answer to an unknown question. Neither responded. Remaining mute for what seemed an eternity I broke the silence. "If you're agreeable, I'd like to arrange a time and place to meet and go over a biographical storyline from you, Mr. Blizzard, and a record of Lt. Blizzard's military history from you, General Walters. We could either meet together or independently."

Mr. Blizzard reached into his overcoat breast pocket and removed a piece of paper and small pen. Using my shoulder as a desktop he scribbled down his address and phone number. "Give me a call next week," he said. "We'll set up a time to get together. General Walters handed me a business card with his administrative number. Give Sergeant Major Rawlings a call at headquarters sometime after you meet with Mr. Blizzard. "We'll talk then." I thanked them, turned, and started toward the exit.

Making my way from Lt. Blizzard's gravesite the landscape gave way to painful remembrances of too many wars. Too numerous to count were the white marble headstones. Each stood in perfect formation on the surrounding hillside, giving the impression of being called to attention by a superior officer. It was a sight that was difficult to grasp yet beautifully disturbing. I knew that there under every stone lay countless tales of an extraordinary hero. The inscription on each stone gave only name, rank, heroic achievements and identification number. A date of birth and death told the brief story of the fallen warrior with God their only witness to each soldier's death and glory.

CHAPTER 2
AN AMERICAN TALE BEGINS

As always, my day started with a glance at my calendar. The 15th was circled in red. Written in bold was **Blizzard 302-667-3471. American Indian story**. I reached for the phone, dialed the number, and waited. No response after several rings. I was about to put the receiver back in the cradle when someone picked up. "Hello, Charlie speaking."

"Mr. Blizzard, this is Bill Waterman. We met at your son's funeral."

"Yes, Mr. Waterman, I've been waiting for your call. I've gathered all of Eddie's personal and military items for you. Citations, medals, letters, and all the personal items sent home to me from the Marine Corps. Everything was cleaned and neatly packed in individual packages in his footlocker and duffle bag. His watch, wallet, clothes, both military and civilian, several diaries, and a number of letters from Rose Ann, a young woman he was seeing. He dated her since grammar school. They were engaged. You're really going to be surprised." I figured the letters must be from the young woman at Eddie's funeral.

His father went on. "Eddie was a note taker. Kept a diary of all his memories from the time he was a child until his death." He paused then

said, "If you have time… drive on up."

It was just what I wanted to hear! "All I need are the directions."

"The address is 27 Pinebury Avenue, Camden, Delaware. You'll take a dirt road off Route 13, south of town. Once you pass through Dover, you'll see a sign on the right that says 'Camden.' Instead of going right into Camden turn left at the next intersection. Second house on the left. White house with red shutters. See you in about three hours or so?"

"Yes, I'll leave now." After saying my good byes I grabbed my briefcase and checked its contents quickly. Slipping into my heavy down jacket I headed for the garage. I was going to get my story! As I reached the garage, I stopped as I always do to admire the car of my dreams, my 1965 Mustang convertible. That was my baby and we covered a lot of ground and a lot of stories together. It was Ford's answer to a lot of people's dreams and my answer to the poor man's sport car. I backed out of the garage and headed north, leaving Washington in my rear view mirror.

It wasn't long before I was driving along Route 300 into the Maryland countryside. The farmlands and surrounding woodlands were lightly covered by snow from the night before. Everything looked virgin and untouched. As I drove along the narrow roadway my mind raced wildly thinking about how I would bring together my powerful and extraordinary story about a native-born Indian who gave his life for this country.

People have little interest in military heroism, and the war in Viet Nam

is becoming a political nightmare. It wasn't unusual to hear of servicemen being attacked by marauding thugs only because they wore the uniforms of their individual services. These same soldiers who fight gallantly in battle are now afraid to walk alone or wear their uniforms for fear of attack. It's a crazy, mixed up climate. Lt. Blizzard's story needs to be told as he was truly an American hero, regardless of what the tone or mood of the public might be at the moment.

Lawlessness is common in most major cities. Longhaired barefoot hippies trying to reach "enlightenment" through the use of smoking pot and hash, and taking LSD, burn the American Flag and publicly destroy their Draft Cards. Young men are protesting by the hundreds and refuse to answer the call to serve their country. Their true passion is hatred of authority and anyone who has anything to do with the war.

Countless numbers of youth are taking flight to the north and the safety of the Canadian borders. Viet Nam War activists, draft dodgers, and deserters take advantage of Canada's liberal Prime Minister Pierre Trudeau's offerings. His famous declaration, stating his country is a Place of Refuge for those who refuse to serve in the U.S. Military means insulation from prosecution and safety from extradition for draft dodgers.

Those deserters apprehended by federal authorities are turned over to their respective services for action under military law. Desertion in wartime could bring the death penalty, but most of these individuals face court marital before being sent to detention centers for a number of months and dishonorably discharged. All will leave their penal colonies with the stig-

ma of being disgracefully released, but for many it doesn't seem to matter.

Chaos is breaking the will of our people, the back of President Lyndon Johnson, and indirectly aiding our enemies. The NVA and their leadership know we are winning the battles in the fields and mountains of their homeland and figure if they can engage us in a lengthy war, victory will be theirs. 1st Lt. Blizzard, 29 years of age, has been confronting the enemy these past months knowing little of what was happening back home. Maybe his story will help turn the tide and make our country unite behind a cause again.

CHAPTER 3
DOVER BOUND

It took just a little over three hours to pass through Dover and then to the by-pass road to Camden. Making the turn off highway 13 onto Pinebury I saw the little white house with red shutters. I knew the Blizzards were of humble origin, as it appeared to be a simple four-room home.

Before I could fully step out of my vehicle, the front door to the little house opened with a thud as the screen door hit the side of the house. Eddie's father stepped out. A large man more than six feet in height with broad shoulders, thick arms, and the facial features of an Apache Indian. High cheekbones, dark brown eyes, and long dark hair. The sun accented the stands of silver from crown to end. His hair was drawn back behind his head in a ponytail.

As we shook hands, my hand was engulfed by his. In fact, his hands were enormous. His grip was strong and tight as if he were passing an unspoken message, telling me that he was the stronger individual.

"Come in, Mr. Waterman, and welcome to our home." He introduced me to his wife Nancy. Offering me a seat on the couch he took the seat opposite me, a seat that offered a commanding position over a guest. Eddie's

mother asked if I wanted anything to drink.

"Water would be fine." I wondered why she wasn't at the funeral. I would let time pass and allow the path to surface before drawing any conclusions or asking any questions.

We sat quietly for a short time before entering into any chit chat. Soon Eddie's personal items were scattered before us. Some items would not be released to me, like Eddie's clothing, watch, photographs, and wallet. Eddie's father said that I could take pictures of the items. Though the diaries and letters were of unlimited value to the family and were irreplaceable, the man let me take them with the promise that I would take extreme care of each and every item, and to guard them as if they were my own. He wasn't worried about the citations, which he knew could be replaced by Headquarters Marine Corps, and he indicated I could take them with me along with Eddie's diaries and letters.

As time passed Eddie's father talked about his son and the many memories they shared together as he watched his son grow from a boy to a man. They had a fire pit in the back yard and he spoke of the fireside counsels he had with his son wherein he shared his values with Little Wolf. That was Eddie's Indian name and that is how his father spoke of him. He passed on stories with gestures and expressions used in the ways of his ancient brothers. According to this man, the warmth and glow of the fire brought he and his son together as one, and they were comfortable with each other as they spoke of the past and future.

At one such event the gift of the pebble came to light. Before each and every long run young warriors were told to place a pebble under their tongue. By doing so, a warrior could run for miles without the need of water. The secret he was told was to drink the saliva from beneath your tongue and never be thirsty. Legend and fact have it that an Apache warrior could run 20 miles without stopping and was quicker on foot than a soldier on horseback. Eddie, his dad said, always placed a pebble in his mouth before playing basketball and football games in both high school and college, where he became a star halfback.

His father said he taught Eddie that the boy would never go hungry if he watched the animals and birds, and ate what they ate. He taught him how to find water in the cactus. It was all in the diary, the man told me with steady, quiet words. As I looked into the eyes of this large, peaceful man I caught a glimpse of what it was to be an Apache Indian in yesteryear and how it was to be one in today's modern world.

I stayed with Eddie's parents for three hours that day, learning what I could about the American Indian hero. What I didn't know was just how real this young man would become to me. I gathered his diaries and other items, thanked his parents for their time and walked to my car. As I loaded all of Eddie's possessions, I felt as if I were being watched, but no one was near me. The old couple wasn't at their door. It was just me, my car and Eddie's memories. I was ready to begin the return trip home. Tomorrow I would begin putting together the story of a remarkable and extraordinary Marine whose life ended before it really began.

CHAPTER 4
A SIMPLE MAN'S LIFE

The following morning I woke up early. As I sat in my office I began the day by placing in chronological order the material that Eddie's father had given me. Using a long folding table I worked from left to right with the earliest years on the left. I laid things out until the last entry Lt. Blizzard made in his diary, dated February 15, 1966.

Most of Eddie's early entries were poorly written and of little interest. However, there were some pages too important to be neglected. Omitting historical data regarding the family migration east would leave open too many unanswered questions. Their forefathers' forced migration and transition to the east in small groups by the U.S. Military would give light as to why an Apache came to live in a small eastern town of less than 1,500 people.

Eddie's diary held a story that was of true interest. It gave me particular insight into the man. The entry was from when he was about 10 years of age and said that his father called him to his side and asked him to sit with him by the fire. It was the summer of 1953 on a warm, clear, moonlit night. Eddie's father told him that his people came from northwestern Canada around 850 A.D., migrating south into the three desert regions:

The Great Basin, The Sonoran, and The Chihuahuas.

Of the six great tribes they were part of the White Mountain Apache who now occupy the lands in southeastern Arizona. Their spoken tongue, Eddie learned that night, was the Athabscan language, which originated during the time they lived in the far north. The tribe's name came from the Zunis who called them Apache. Literal translation? "Enemy."

"For many years we lived in peaceful relations with our neighboring tribes and peoples," Eddie's father told him. "When the Spaniards arrived everything changed. They needed workers for the silver mines that they found in the White Mountains and to the west. Our people were taken to the mines as prisoners and sentenced to labor under the worst conditions. Little water and even less food sapped our people's energy and desire to live."

The diary entry went further, saying that living in harmony with the Spaniards ended and they in turn began to feel the pain of the Apaches' knives and arrows. "We stole their horses, their cattle, their weapons, and took many captives," explained Eddie's father. "We used them like the Spaniards used our people, and like the Whites used the Blacks."

I was captivated by the words I read as I continued.

"Your great grandfather's raiding parties were not undertaken out of necessity, but chiefly for revenge and re-supply. Our forefathers needed horses, guns, and food. For the most part they wanted the Spaniards and

Whites to suffer the wrongs that our people had suffered. At that time in history, the name Apache struck fear into everyone's hearts who lived in the southwest, even the Mexicans. We gave no mercy. We asked for no mercy. An eye for an eye as the Whites would say."

I checked the facts. It was true what Eddie's father was telling him. By the early 1800s the Apache were raiding the Mexican territories and westbound American settlers. Under Chiricahua leaders, Cochise, Mangas Coloradas, Victorio, and a great warrior named Geronimo their battles continued until the surrender of Geronimo and Juh in 1886.

The diary entry continued. Eddie's father told him, "In March of 1886 General George Crook, U.S. Army, managed a meeting with Chiefs Juh and Geronimo. They surrendered and agreed to a two-year imprisonment in Fort Marion 2,000 miles away in Florida. While en route to Fort Bowie, Geronimo, my father, my mother and several others escaped. Months later they were caught again by General Nelson Miles, Crook's replacement. After processing most of the captives several hundred of our people were placed on a train destined for Ft. Marion, an old Spanish fortress in St. Augustine, Florida. It was here where the most dangerous Apaches would serve out their terms of punishment.

"After days of travel cramped up in a boxcar your grandfather, grandmother, and another man and woman jumped the train as it slowed to stop in a small town for supplies. Hiding by day, wandering northeast by night, they foraged off the land and eventually found their way to a small farm in Wyoming, Delaware. The Spirits were good to them. They were given

refuge and hope by a family named McGee who were Irish immigrants. It was here they worked. It was here I was born. It was here that I married your mother, the child of the other couple that had escaped with us that eventful evening."

I put the diary entry back on the table. What a great story. I knew it was all coming together now.

CHAPTER 5
ANY BOY'S STORY

As I learned about Eddie, the man, I wondered how he came to be Eddie the hero from such humble beginnings. How did this young man who didn't do well in school and who didn't stand out aside from being a star athlete turn into such an outstanding marine. I needed to look into Eddie's schooling more. Maybe I was missing something. An athlete like Eddie should have earned a scholarship, but he didn't. Why? It became a consuming question.

Eddie attended Caesar Rodney High School. I learned that Caesar Rodney's school district had always gleaned its students from the neighboring area. All come from a radius of about 15 miles at the most. The school stands on approximately 15 acres of land with three individual buildings. All three are interconnected by bridge ways, which are located on the second floor of each building, giving easy access from one structure to another. On the surrounding grounds are a baseball field, football field, and two tennis courts. The center building is the senior high school and focal point of the campus. On the left of center is the elementary school, on the right the junior high. All the administrative offices, gymnasium, and assembly hall are in the high school structure. The school was named after Caesar Rodney, a member of the Delaware Assembly who rode 80 miles through a thunderstorm on the night of July 1, 1776, to Philadelphia to sign the Declaration of Independence, thus separating all ties with British Parliament and the King of England. From that famous ride came the nicknames for the attendees of the school, Caesar Rodney Rider or Caesar Rodney Riders.

The overall student body from grades one through 12 is small in number. This led the School Board to mutually agree that the primary grades should be united. First and second grades, third and fourth grades, and then fifth and sixth grades would be taught together. The seventh and eighth intermediate grades or junior high are linked somewhat and take a few classes together. The freshmen through senior class receive their studies in individual classrooms depending on the type – Math, English, Science, or the Arts – and move from class to class every hour. The average number of students per class ranges from 15 to 25 students depending on the course.

All students are encouraged to participate in school activities. School Board policy makes it impossible for any individual to be cut from any club or sport for any reason except disrupting the activity itself. The students may participate in any sport, but are not required to play in any game if in the opinion the coaching staff the student could be seriously injured or is not qualified to play ahead of a more qualified athlete.

Eddie's role has been the starting tailback on the freshman football team. The stats he put on the board lead the coaches to decide that as a sophomore he would be called up to the Varsity Squad. He was big, strong, quick on his feet, and violent as a runner. It took more than one defensive back to bring him down once he broke through the line. By the time he was in his junior year he held a number of records at Caesar Rodney for yards per game, yards per punt and kick-off returns. He defensively led the team in tackles as a free safety. As his father taught him, he played with a pebble under his tongue. Offensively and defensively he was outstanding. He didn't just love the game of football he lived it every day of his life. In the classroom his mind would wander to the game he loved so much.

Midway through his junior year a number of colleges had contacted the coaches about Eddie's personal habits. They already knew his game was above average. They wanted to know if he was liked by his teammates. Did he work hard at practice? Could he take criticism? How were his grades? Did he work out in the weight room? Most of the answers were yes, except for grades, which were below average. Plus, Eddie didn't work out in the weight room. He would have, but the Athletic Department couldn't afford to purchase barbells, weights, benches, etc., so there wasn't any weight room. Most of the student athletes were farm boys who worked all summer, day after day, building body strength from manual labor. These kids worked hard, played hard, and gave it their best.

At the end of every year the last game was against their archrival, Dover High School. Crowd attendance for their home games might be 200 people. For the CR/Dover game it was standing room only. Football scouts from the Tri-State Area colleges and universities were always in attendance looking for players to add to their rosters. The game was a dogfight to the bitter end with the score usually ending within a few points of each other. A field goal, a missed extra point; it was always that close.

When the Caesar Rodney Riders ran onto the field in their patched-up, faded, 5-year-old blue and gold jerseys it looked as if the contest was already over. The school's Athletic Department hadn't purchased any equipment or uniforms for years. No money. The spoiled city guys with new dark blue and white uniforms issued the day before the big game looked the part, but before game's end they usually took on the look of the farms boys... soiled and grubby. Two teams hitting, pushing, and struggling with each other for a full 48 minutes was what the crowd came to see. By the time it was over very few in the stadium were disappointed. It just so happened that the Riders won this year by a field goal scoring the victory in the waning moments: 10 to 7!

DIARY ENTRY
September 1959

Today is the 5th, and school started with most of the kids signing up for their standard grade-level classes. It's nice seeing my classmates and all the familiar faces. I've been away most of the summer working the fields in Felton. Sometimes I'd see a few of the guys and gals swimming at Joseph's Lake in Wyoming on a Sunday when I came home to see my parents.

At registration I signed up for English, which I hate, Political Science, Chemistry, U. S. History, Art, and Algebra II, which I flunked last year. I also signed up for Study Hall and Gym. Study Hall can't hurt. I had to keep a C average or I wouldn't be playing football this season. Wanted to go to summer school, but had to work for Mr. Greenwell and needed the money for college. Coach Brown, my Algebra teacher told me he'd tutor me this year. He'll probably give me a D so I remain eligible to play and able to graduate with my class in June. I'm going to try for a better grade, but Algebra is tough.

***

During registration today I saw Rose Ann, the girl of my dreams. I've liked this gal ever since grammar school. Mom and Dad call it puppy love, but for me it's been authentic, genuine, and sincere ever since the day we met. Our dilemma has been our age difference. We met when I was 10 and she was eight. I was in fifth grade; she was in third. Now

our age difference doesn't mean so much. She's a sophomore and 15; I'm a senior and 17. She's a cute blond with a beautiful figure. She's pretty! Her smile takes my breath away. I know she likes me and I know she knows I like her. I want to ask her out, but I'm afraid she might say no. I'd hate that. Like my friends always say, sometimes I'm too shy for my own good.

Rose Ann and I smile at each other as we pass in the hall. We sit next to each other at assemblies. We sit together at the same table for lunch. Accidentally and deliberately we touch each other's shoulders as we pass in the hall. Even by design when in study hall our hands touch with the passing of a book, a sheet of paper, a notebook, anything that brings us together for even a short moment. Now that I think about it, maybe I should just ask her out. She likes me.

I heard Rose Ann ask Mrs. Bailey, the school's Registration Governess, what study hall I had been assigned. Mrs. Bailey knew that students that had crushes on each other often try to get classes together if it can be arranged. I assumed she knew it was the only class we could share together, since she was a sophomore and I was a senior. It was pretty nice of her to assign us the same period for study hall. May the spirits bless her soul.

Wish I could get up enough nerve to ask Rose Ann to be my date at the Back-to-School Dance on the 12th. It's on the day after our opening football game with Milford. Believe me, my heart leaps out of my chest every time she passes me or is near me. I've made a pledge to myself that forever and a day I'll carry this flame and someday tell her how much she has meant to me. I want to tell her I've felt this way for many years. I've got to do something soon or some other guy will take her to the dance.

***

Our football team has been practicing daily for the past few weeks. As always, the linemen start the practice by dragging an enormous sled around the perimeter of the field. Each sled has four 100-pound bags of sand. Every lineman has to drag it around the field three times. While they're doing that the wide receivers and running backs are doing wind sprint – painful, agonizing, excruciating, gut wrenching wind sprints. Most of us would rather be pulling the sled than duplicating sprint after sprint. Coach Brown learned all these conditioning drills at a coach's clinic in Philadelphia one summer from Penn State Coach Fazio. His staff was first-rate to our coaching staff when they gifted us their playbooks on the T formation. The T formation if run properly is a thorny problem for any defense. Coach Brown plans for us to use it in our opening game against Milford High on the 11th. Everything is coming along fine.

***

Rose Ann is on the cheerleading squad, so I see her during football practice. She doesn't know it, but I watch her as they practice cheers on the nearby tennis courts. It's difficult for me not to, but Coach Brown keeps me in line. He keeps reminding me to keep my mind on the game and punishes me by making me pull the sled one time around the field every time I look in her direction. Regardless of how many times I have to pull that sled, I'm taking my chances. I can't help myself. Coach Brown knows what's going on between us and is probably laughing his guts out each time he assigns me another trip around the field. Sometimes I'm there till dark pulling that sled. I promised myself today is the day I'm asking Rose Ann to the dance. Right after practice, if she's by herself and no one else is around, I'm going to ask her to the dance. Maybe!

***

Our football team has been outstanding so far this year. Attribute it to the new formations we're using. The Varsity is 5-0; the JV squad is 4-1. Tonight we have a home game against Seaford High. The number of our fans improves with every win. Their record is 4-1, losing only to Dover, our main rival. All our coaches say it will be a hard-fought game and that the winner will be decided in the fourth quarter. All of us are to load up on pasta prior to any game. It's supposed to do something to give us added strength as the game goes on. I've never noticed any difference, but if the coaches say eat pasta, we eat pasta. The only thing I do different from the rest of my teammates is placing that pebble under my tongue. I think it makes a difference.

Several college recruiters have been attending our practices and talking to Coach Brown lately. As our season draws to a close the recruiters seem to be focusing on three guys... Ryan Gardner, our tight end,

Jason Bradley a split end, and an unknown running back. Coach won't say who it is, but I'm pretty sure it's me. At CR I hold just about every record for an offensive running back, I'm above average on defense, and I've got the size and speed. The Wilmington Journal and Dover Times have had several write-ups about the CR Riders and the stats I'm rolling up per game. I'm hopeful the University of Delaware will give me a scholarship, and if they do I'll use the money I've banked in Wyoming to buy a car. The driving distance from Newark to Camden is only an hour, which will give me the opportunity to come home on weekends to see Rose Ann, my secret love. I don't know if she really understands how I feel about her!

CHAPTER 6
RACCOONS AND FRIENDS

Eddie did finally get the nerve up to ask Rose Ann to the back-to-school dance. They'd been seeing each other regularly the past few weeks. According to Eddie's Diary, Rose Ann's brother Vic wasn't too pleased with his sister's choice in a boyfriend but was too small in stature and physique to do anything about it. Besides, he and Eddie had been hunting and fishing buddies since they were in grammar school. Over the years Vic repeatedly gained knowledge about survival from Eddie. He learned how to make fishing hooks out of the ribs of mice and how to catch a raccoon using only a gallon jug with a finger ring, six feet of rope, and a small ball of aluminum foil. These skills amazed me. I wanted to learn more.

Eddie told him a raccoon travels identical pathways over and over in the pursuit of water to cleanse his food. Finding his trail's end at water's edge you set your trap. First, he told him to roll the aluminum foil into a miniature ball and place it into the jug. Second, secure one end of the six-foot rope to a neighboring tree while connecting the other end to the ring at the neck of the jug. Finally, position the jug at water's edge while disguising the rope with leaves and branches from the surrounding area.

Unable to resist the shiny aluminum ball inside the jar, any raccoon that passed by would stick his tiny hand inside in an attempt to steal its contents. Once his fist closes around the tiny ball, he's powerless to exit his hand from the jar as it larger than the exit hole. Repeatedly he'll attempt to get his fist from the jar but his obsession with stealing the foil imprisons him. The raccoon becomes attached to the jar forever unless someone sets him free.

According to diary entries, the boys' first attempt captured a rather large raccoon. Exhausted from continuous attempts to escape he still had enough energy in reserve to let them know he was in a very nasty mood. They threw a blanket over the brute and physically held him to the ground. Shattering the jar at the neck of the bottle with a small hammer Eddie carried in his waist band it took less than five seconds for the enraged beast to scamper from beneath the blanket and sprint out of sight.

It was clear that Vic liked Eddie, but Eddie dating his sister was another issue. Part of the reason was Eddie's race, but Vic's love for his sister was undeniable. If Eddie made her happy, he'd keep his mouth shut. That didn't mean the townspeople would go along with the program. Rose Ann didn't care. She knew Eddie as a decent human being and not as a dark-skinned savage. As a result, her home was egged from time to time by a group of kids she went to school with as an act of discrimination.

Eddie didn't own a car, and his Dad refused to let him use the family Buick for dating purposes. As a result, Rose Ann and Eddie would meet at a pre-arranged place using their bicycles for transportation. Most of the time they'd meet at the Wyoming Mill Pond, they'd sit together, talk about everything and anything, and sometimes just hold hands while they listened to the water as it cascaded over a nearby waterfall. There by that waterfall, just as the sun was setting on the horizon, they had their first awkward kiss. Who initiated that moment remains unresolved. Eddie said she did. Later, Rose Ann would tell him that he did. Regardless, they were delighted it happened. It was that very moment that they would both commit to memory for the remainder of their lives. But that was just one intimate detail I learned from Eddie's writings. He was an interesting man with an intriguing history.

For example, Eddie worked on a farm in Felton, Delaware, every summer. Beginning his freshman year and until graduating from Caesar Rodney, he laboriously worked his summers away under the hot sun. The physical labor of dragging baskets of fruit, vegetables, and bales of alfalfa for the three-month summer growing periods began to show in Eddie's muscle mass. Each year he grew larger. His shoulders became wider, neck thicker, arms and legs more imposing. He grew into an impressive specimen of a young man. With each passing football season he was heavier, stronger, and faster than the year before. Anyone who talked to Coach Brown knew he was anxious to see how much more weight Eddie had put on before the new school year and if his speed had decreased after the added weight and hard summers in Felton.

Eddie told friends that he worked more for the exercise than for the $12.00 a week. Of course he wanted the money as he wanted to go to the local college in Dover. He always said that Wellington College was his dream come true. The first Indian in his family to get a college education. That's what it meant. If only he would concentrate more on his studies and less on formations, patterns, and holes created by the linemen for him to run through, but that was Eddie. That's what his father told me during our meeting anyway.

Greenwell, the owner of the farm gave him a summer job with room and board, and told him to stay away from his daughters or he'd send him packing. Eddie's diary stated clearly that he wasn't interested in this man's "unsightly" daughters. All he wanted was a job for the summer and to save money to go to school. Greenwell worked him six days a week from sunrise to sunset, and made him go to church with his family every Sunday. After church Eddie was free to do what he wished.

On the Greenwell farm lived several families that were descendents of slaves. Set free by proclamation after the Civil War they had nowhere to go. Several generations of these families had been on this farm their entire lives. They were devoted to the Greenwell family as laborers, cooks and housekeepers. The Greenwell family gave them a number of acres to grow their own foodstuff and stay on in the old original one-room wooden houses. Since the day of emancipation they've remained on this farm as workers for pay and subsistence.

According to Eddie's father, he would go to one families' home, sit with them on their stoop on Sundays after church, listen to their folklore, and be in awe of their history. He shared the stories with his father. He said that he couldn't believe what they had gone through.

Leon, the master of his family, stood about six feet tall and was extremely muscular from years of toil in the fields. His voice was something to behold, loud, strong, and clear, equal to any Tenor he had ever heard. He would lead his family and groups of workers in singing many of the old tribal spirituals as they toiled in the fields. Work for Eddie became more of an activity than a task when listening to the verses in their native tongue. He always wondered if they understood the words they were singing. Not understanding a word was immaterial to Eddie. It was the melody that brought significance to the moment. It helped him work.

I was captivated by an entry in Eddie's diaries that told about how Leon owned a rabbit dog that had a litter of puppies. Eddie asked if any were for sale and if he could buy one of his prize pups. Since they were such good friends and Leon liked the young man, he refused any payment and gave Eddie the pick of the litter. The boy selected the most active, excitable, tail-wagging Beagle pup in the box. He named him Rubic and trained him the winter of '58. People got used to seeing the dog, and wherever the dog was seen, they'd see Eddie. The two were inseparable.

Every September for three years Eddie deposited $144.00 in cash in the Camden/Wyoming Bank, amassing a grand total of $432.00. That was just enough for a commuting student to go to school for two years. Money earned from long, hard labor. This summer, he also had three months of hair growth over his shoulders, a few extra pounds of muscle, a very dark tan, and was physically ready for football practice and the joy it brought him.

CHAPTER 7
MISSED OPPORTUNITY

I kept reading diary entries. Nothing terribly exciting. Eddie was a very average student and excellent athlete. He finished his senior year at CR. I found no traces of his GPA. All Eddie mentioned in his diary was that he was in the bottom third of his class. Nothing about his grades. I assumed he passed Algebra since he graduated the following June.

The Riders finished their football season 7-0, winning over the Dover Bulldogs 14-3. Unfortunately, as it turned out, Eddie was never offered a scholarship to play football anywhere. Of the 15 colleges and universities that had initial interest in him only the University of Delaware continued to offer him encouragement. His teammates, Ryan Gardner and Jason Bradley, received scholarships. Gardner went to Penn State University and Bradley to the University of Mississippi. Eddie expressed being happy for them but heartbroken nothing came his way. He was definitely an outstanding athlete that needed to make several changes in his life. A lot of diary entries were devoted to his weighing out his options, which were limited at best. Wellington was a local college. He decided he might have a chance there.

Eddie was told by University of Delaware Recruiter Greg McDonald to gain admittance to Wellington. After one year if his grades improved to a 2.5 GPA they would reconsider him in the fall of 1961. That was the only reference to his actual grades.

McDonald told Eddie that at this time that the University of Delaware would not offer him a scholarship due to unacceptable grades. They knew about him and it was obvious that he was more interested in leisure activities with his girlfriend than working for good grades. His overall academics and focus on school needed much improvement. Everything else seemed to fall in line with what they wanted in a student athlete at the university and that Eddie's character was unquestionable. He was never in trouble at school or with the law, and his talent on the gridiron was certainly something they wanted in their program at the University of Delaware, but his grades... Wellington would help get Eddie on track.

In early July Eddie submitted an application to Wellington for the fall semester. His application was reviewed, accepted, forwarded, and dated August 1, 1960. The Dean of Students enclosed within the letter of acceptance a communication accepting him on academic probation for the fall semester. A personal interview with the Dean in his office had to be acknowledged and finalized before Eddie would be able to schedule any classes. If the Dean found him to be focusing on academics he would endorse his application.

Dean Sterling also informed Eddie that the NCAA had documented his SAT scores and GPA, informing the school that he was above the minimum standards for participation in any Wellington sports program.

"Eligible to play," as it's called. Wellington's only prerequisites, limitations, or stipulations would be that Eddie sign up for and actually attend a mandatory study group, arrange and sign a contract with a seasoned tutor that was acceptable to the Dean, and have the Dean's personal authorization prior to attending any football activities.

Eddie would never know the amount of time the Athletic Department spent in petitioning the Dean's consent on his behalf. Finally convinced they could use him as an advertising tool for general admission the Dean would allow Eddie to play football while on academic probation. The college's Coach Hackett gave Eddie his personal phone number so they could arrange an interview at the earliest possible date, one that would coincide with Dean Sterling's meeting.

The interviews with the Dean of Students and Coach Hackett went well. They held one meeting in the morning with the Dean and the other in the afternoon with Coach Hackett. He was approved and accepted by both that day. Eddie would be allowed to enroll. He became a freshman in the Class of '64 and unknowingly was penciled in as the starting tailback on the Wolverine Football team. All this in one day and without one minute of practice.

Coach Hackett immediately arranged for Eddie to report to school as soon as he could make himself available. His room assignment was in the wing of the dorm that housed all current and new incoming student athletes. There was an upperclassman named William Cohan, an honor student, assigned to the same room as Eddie's. Cohan would be his roommate and was to be mentor, advisor, and the person providing secret reports to the coaching staff in regard to Eddie's study habits. Coach Hackett arranged a soft academic schedule for his first semester and informed him of a scheduled meeting the team was having on evening of the 10th at 7:30 p.m. Eddie's college studies and passion for football were about to begin once again.

Many of the players knew of Eddie Blizzard before he attended the team meeting. They had read about him in the local papers and some had seen him play, but no one expected him to be attending Wellington. Most thought he would get a scholarship to a major university and never dreamed he would be their teammate. Most were pleased with his addition to the team… everyone but the running backs. They would be challenging Eddie at the tailback position and knew they were about to be placed on special teams or the bench.

Eddie's diary entries fell off for a period of time. I thought maybe he was busy with football and girls, but the next entry caught me by surprise. He didn't get a scholarship. He was passed over in a big way. Eddie's weakness caught up with him and changed his life. Poor grades and bad study habits meant Eddie would have to choose an alternate path in life. Like so many young men in his situation, he would go military.

DIARY ENTRY
September 1962

On Monday, September 9, I entered a U.S. Marine Corps recruiter's office in Darby, Pennsylvania. It had been my intention to sign up for only two years of active service. I left his office signing a four-year commitment.

Someone told me that the Marine Corps administers tests to evaluate and determine an area of special programs for each recruit. These test scores place you in a category or MOS or Military Occupational Specialty for placements or assignments. Knowing their importance I went to the library, checked out all the publications I could on improving one's IQ score and general aptitude test scores. For the first time in my life I studied for several weeks before an exam and aced the aptitude test! I scored 121 on the IQ exam. A score of 120 was required for any officer core curriculum. I was hoping I would qualify for just one program leading to an officer's commission.

Only days after passing the exams and signing the papers my recruiter called and told me to meet him on Sunday, September 15, in front of Penn Central Station, downtown Philly. Muster at 0930 military time. He said, "Do not be late."

Dad drove me to Darby that day, placed me on the trolley to Penn Central, and 45 minutes later I met the only Marine I knew in the world, my recruiter. He handed me a packet, and told me my orders were inside. "Do not open the packet." Memorizing the 11 General Orders printed on the back of the packet by the time you arrive in Yamassee, South Carolina, your soon-to-be new home. He handed me my one-way ticket, gave me my instructions to train and track number, and told me I would be met by a Sergeant Wilcox at Yamassee. He wished me good luck.

Fifteen hours later, around 2 a.m., as I stepped off the train onto the platform. A figure came running out of the darkness screaming at the top of his lungs, "Recruits, get your asses over here, shut your fucking mouths, don't say a word, or I'll have you castrated right here on this platform without the use of an anesthetic. Show me your unopened orders. If they are opened you have signed your death warrant. If they are opened go 20 paces to my right and wait. If they are unopened get on the green bus to my left!" Not a single recruit had opened his packet.

The bus ride from Yamassee to Parris Island was quiet, uneventful, and not a word was spoken by anyone. It was if I had been swallowed up in the darkness. As we passed through the gates at Parris Island I remember saying to myself, "Eddie you just made the biggest mistake of your life." But there was no turning back.

Stopping in front of Building 361, the receiving barracks for new re-cruits, the screaming started again. "Get out of my bus. Get in the building. Stand by twos in front of the racks. Go, go, go! I found myself running. We recruits learned quickly that "racks" were rows of beds stacked one on top of the other. The racks were equally spaced apart and lined up on both sides of the squad bay, our new home. The center of the squad bay was an open area 20 paces wide, an area the Drill Instructor used to spit out the venom he needed to poison our useless little brains.

I noticed at the far end of the squad bay there stood a Marine about five foot ten, weighing about 180 pounds, of muscular build, wearing a Smoky Bear hat. His uniform shirt and trousers were without a wrinkle or mark. The mark was across his face. This Marine had a scar running across his forehead down and over his left eye that stopped about mid cheek. Above the left breast pocket he wore three rows of ribbons, probably representing campaigns he had fought in and rewards for valor in combat. The only ribbon I recognized was the Purple Heart. Above the ribbons he wore Jump Wings or Aircrew Wings. This guy had been around.

You could hear a pin drop throughout the barracks when this Marine stepped forward and started talking. "I am your Senior Drill Instructor. My name is Gunnery Sergeant MedVecky. I have been in my beloved Marine Corps for 18 years. I love the Corps. You will not fuck with my Corps. If you do, I will have you executed. From this moment on, the first word out of your mouth will be 'Sir' and the last word will be 'Sir.' Do you maggots understand?"

We all answered in unison, "Sir, yes, Sir."

Moving slowly down the squad bay the instructor continued his in-

troduction. *"You will not like me. I do not give a shit. You will learn to hate me. I do not care. I am not here to take care of you. I am not your mother. I am here to teach you to be a predator. If you screw up as a member of this platoon; Platoon 362, I will personally tear your balls off so you will never reproduce. Believe me when I say I am not prejudiced. I do not have an unfavorable opinion of any of you. I treat Niggers, Jews, Spicks, Dagos, Whites, all the same. Like the piece of human shit that you are…"*

Just then he looked at me. "Who the fuck are you looking at asshole?" he screamed. I was speechless. "You look like a fucking Indian? Are you an Indian?"

"Sir, yes, Sir!"

"What kind of Indian are you?"

"Apache, Sir."

"Where you from?"

"Delaware, Sir."

"Apaches are from Arizona. What the fuck are you doing in Delaware? You get lost?"

He asked so many questions so quickly that I didn't have time to answer.

"What's your name Indian?" he said.

"Blizzard, Sir. Eddie Blizzard."

"You got an Indian name?"

"Little Wolf, Sir."

"You look like Little Pussy to me!"

From that moment on I knew he was going to call me Little Pussy.

Turning away from me MedVecky continued his walk down the line. Nothing but poisonous obscenities spewed from his mouth. The guy was sick. Suddenly he punched a recruit in the stomach. As the man fell to the floor Sgt. MedVecky screamed at him to get up before he kicked his brains out. At that point I knew Gunnery Sergeant MedVecky was insane.

Of the 70 plus recruits that stood there in this squad bay on the early morning hours of the 16th of September, I was sure MedVecky or one of his "friendly" associates would kill one of us before our recruit training was over.

Sunday, September 28, 1962

Have had little opportunity to make any entries for the past two weeks. MedVecky introduced us to three additional associates: Sergeants Stein, Gallagher, and Maxwell. All three are mentally deranged. Our pain is now multiplied by four.

The first few days in training involved getting our assignments to permanent living quarters, physical exams, shots, haircuts, initial uniform allowance, our 782 gear (we learned this means field equipment), footlockers, buckets, and silver helmets. We accomplished this with four madmen screaming at the top of their lungs every step of the way. We're beat.

Of the four DIs, MedVecky is the Senior Drill Instructor. His purpose in life is to destroy our spirit, vigor, and reason to be alive. He is offensive, despicable, depraved, and wholeheartedly mentally ill. He is a sick individual. A twisted piece of perverted humanity. He's one step below the other three.

Sgt. Maxwell marched us to the parade field tonight just before Sunset. Told us that if we stood motionless for 30 minutes, and if we let the mosquitoes and gnats feed on us without moving from the position of attention, he'd take us to a movie. He called it "Ambush Training." We did it. Not a recruit moved the entire time as mosquitoes and no-see-ums crawled in our ears, noses, etc. For 30 minutes we let the bugs eat us alive. Sgt. Maxwell kept his word. The asshole took us to a movie on the M-1 rifle. Our platoon will be going to the rifle range tomorrow.

Lectures on safety took up a good portion of this evening. What to do what not to do. Most important, firing our weapons would begin only when the Drill Instructor says, "safeties off. All ready on the right, all ready on the left, all clear on the firing range, commence firing." Anyone firing his weapon without the all clear would have his trigger finger removed in a most painful way and therefore be of little use to the Corps. Wonder what MedVecky meant by that. Firing will stop when given the command "Cease fire, safeties on." Most anxious to get started.

Wrote a letter to Mom and girlfriend. That broke up the monotony a bit, but then it was back to training.

Arriving at the rifle range MedVecky instructed us to gather around in a semi circle. Facing us with the targets in the distant background, he began by saying, "Today is an important day in your life. You will learn to be the most dangerous weapon in the world... a Marine and his M-1." Taking a weapon from a recruit MedVecky said, "Your M-1 is an air cooled, gas operated, clip-fed, semi-automatic shoulder weapon. Its effective Range is 500 yards. Each clip holds 8 rounds. Your weapon weighs 9.5 pounds and is 43.6 inches long. With this weapon in your hands and after you have learned to use it, you will be an instrument of death. Every round that you fire will be on a journey... a journey to kill."

He didn't stop there. "In the near future you will be going to Nam. Look at me!" He pointed to his cheek and tapped it a couple of times.

"I struggled with a man whose only goal at that moment was to kill me. Someday you will come face to face with your enemy as I did. At that moment you will either kill him or he will kill you. Do not hesitate. If you do you will be a dead Marine. You will come home in a body bag. One of the two dog tags you have been issued will be in your mouth wedged between your two front teeth; the other will be around your neck. At that point you will be of no use to your platoon, company, or battalion. You will be a piece of rotting shit. Before that happens, kill your enemy. Let him die for his country. You live for yours. Now, line up in pairs of twos in front of the numbered markers down the line. Move, maggots, move." Thus our training began.

For the next four days I fired my 50 rounds per day of ammo. My groups of hits inched closer and closer to the bullseye and when qualification day arrived I fired a 238 out of a possible 250. There were only 10 of us who fired expert. Much to our surprise and unknown to us beforehand, the top four shooters would make the Platoon Rifle Team and would be spending an extra week on the range competing against three other platoons in our battalion. The remainder of the platoon went to mess duty, cleaning dishes, peeling potatoes, and serving food at the mess hall.

After the extra week our team came in second at the battalion competition. Sgt. MedVecky was pissed. Said it made him look bad to the Company Commander and would reflect on his fitness report. Said we were fuck-ups. Made us do 10 sit-ups for every point under 250 each individual shot. Scored 54 points under the max for the four of us, times 10, equaled 540 sit-ups. Private Reddish shot the lowest of our four scores. MedVecky doubled up on his sit-ups and added 20 minutes of running in place. What a guy!

***

Monday, September 29, 1962

0630: Up and about this morning bright eyed and bushy tailed. Med-Vecky hollering and screaming about the three S's. "Thirty minutes to shit, shave, shower and be outside by 0700. No ifs ands or buts. Be in front of the barracks ramrod tall by 0700."

0700: came with the platoon at attention as directed. MedVecky called out for his college boys to fall out of the formation and get our asses up to his office. "Pronto, move, you shit birds!" In the meantime the smoking lamp was lighted for the remainder of the platoon and would be until his return.

Four of us ran to his office wondering what was in his bag of tricks this time. In the past we college boys, as he called us, had to clean the heads, demonstrating to the rest of the platoon what a college education had done for us. Hopefully today would be different.

MedVecky walked into the room and sat down at his desk. We could tell something was up. He looked up at the four of us and asked, "Who wants to be an officer in my Corps? It seems the Marine Corps is out of qualified applicants and has to dig down into the enlisted ranks to fill the quotas. Any of you shit birds interested in going to flight training at Pensacola or going to the Naval Academy at Annapolis?"

Afraid to answer, we all thought it was just another sadistic joke on his college boys. Repeating the question, he added that we had just one minute to answer or get back in formation with the rest of the platoon.

I answered first. "Yes, Sir! I'd like the opportunity to apply for either one."

Waiting for the others to respond and getting no answer MedVecky pointed at the remaining recruits and screamed, "You three numb nuts get out of my office!"

MedVecky stared hard at me like he regarded me as unworthy. I was a recruit in boot camp, and the Corps as far as he was concerned didn't need a misfit trying to squeeze in through the cracks using Marine Corps Orders or Directives just because they had a respectable IQ. I assumed he knew I had the minimum test scores and IQ to qualify for most OCS programs but didn't share my enthusiasm for advancement. I was just another Indian who ought to be riding a pony. I saw it in his eyes. I should not fly an airplane or sit in an engineering classroom. I've heard it all before. MedVecky looked at me. "Just the Corps bad luck, Blizzard. You'll probably pass the exams."

Next thing you know I was following him out of the office like a dog heeling to his master's command. I walked slightly behind and to the left, wondering where we were headed. There in the parking lot adjacent to the barracks was a Jeep waiting to take whomever was ordered or qualified to go to Battalion Headquarters for testing. Staff Sgt. Gorden asked MedVecky if I was the only one. MedVecky replied, "Only one asshole and here he is." Then he turned to me. "Private Blizzard, when you get back from testing, you're in for some real pain."

CHAPTER 8
LETTERS FROM HOME

There on the table before me were a stack of letters from both Eddie's father and the only girl he ever dated, the girl he loved, sweet and beautiful Rose Ann. As I began to read their most private thoughts I felt somewhat like a thief. It however, gave me a better understanding of who they were and what they meant to each other. I began with the letters from Eddie's father.

October 2, 1962

My Dear Son,

It is lonely by the fireside without you. Your warm stories of school, sports, and friends have escaped into the night. I miss them. As I sit here writing this letter I look into the dancing fire and ask the gods to look upon you with pleasure. I pray they give you the faith of our ancestors, to give you pride in yourself, and to let you fear no man. May the sun shine upon you and warm your soul.

Continue to dedicate your life to honor, principle, and freedom.

Remember that you are a tribute from our people to the Marine Corps. Let them see, through you and your actions, what a great people we are. Educate them in our customs, traditions, and way of life. Learn theirs; remember ours.

I know as you read my words you are saying, "My father will in no way bring an end to his guidance and love for me." Eddie, it shall only cease when the Black Horse comes to take me away.

The cutest young woman stopped by today. Her name is Rose Ann, as if I didn't know! Rode here on her bicycle. You're a very lucky man. What a delightful person. She loves you like the night loves the stars.

Rose Ann mentioned you've written her a few letters. She shared one with us. Won't tell you which one, but from what she read to us puppy love has gone the way of the buffalo. Her love for you and your love for her is sincere. She awaits your return.

I received a letter from your Commanding Officer, a Lieutenant Colonel Parks. Says your platoon is making progress. That you will be graduating from recruit training on schedule December 12th. If we are to attend your graduation ceremony we must prepare for it now. Do you want your mother and I to come? Where do you go after Recruit Training? Since it's around Christmas I assume everything from trains to hotels will be booked solid. Maybe we should stay here and await your return. Rose Ann wants you to come home. Her heart is empty while you are away. Let us know your plans.

We are swollen with pride knowing you are to become an officer and pilot in the Marine Corps. You must let you failures at Wellington motivate you to success. The door of opportunity opens only a few times in life. Pass through this portal to victory.

You said in your last letter you are coming home immediately after graduation. We shall await your return here in Camden if you do not want us to come to your graduation ceremony. If you like we will have your friends over to greet you on your return. Rose Ann will definitely be here.

Rubic continues to search the house for you. He sleeps by the front door every night awaiting your return. It has been sad watching his loneliness for you. I took him hunting yesterday thinking the hunt would help. After coming home he again searched the house for you, the shed, the bedrooms, the living room, dining room, everywhere. Unable to find you he returned to the same spot at the front door. He is firm in the belief you will return.

Hope all goes well with you.

As Ever,

October 15, 1962

My Dearest Eddie,

Let me begin by telling you I laughed so hard when you told me how your Drill Instructors have been treating you. I know that might sound cruel of me but I know that no matter what they say or do, their words and deeds only ride off your back like water off a duck. Your background of strength and endurance is something unknown to them as they think you are just another recruit and not the Champion of Strength that you are.

Keep your chin up darling. Before you know it you'll be in Pensacola, undergoing flight training to be a pilot, and Sgt. MedVecky and his cohorts will be a thing of the past. I've been telling all my friends that you were accepted into the Marine Cadet Program to become a pilot. They're happy for you, yet I'm sad as you'll be so far away when you start your classes, and I'll be here at school.

I can't tell you how proud you have made me along with my parents and Vic. We're overjoyed with your achievements at Parris Island and with all you have accomplished in the Marines thus far. This enlistment, though a lengthy four years plus, has motivated you to bigger and better things than football. I accept our separation knowing sooner than later we will be united once again. Can you imagine? An officer in the Corps? I'll wait for you forever.

Your mom and dad are eager to read your letters and await them daily. All of us know you are extremely busy with training and that your free time is limited, but if a day goes by without a letter, we say to ourselves that tomorrow, wait until tomorrow, it will come tomorrow.

We are above all excited about your homecoming. December can't come soon enough. Your gift to me for Christmas can be private time together out at the Mill Pond. I go there often and sit by the waterfall. As the water spills over the dam and continues downstream it works its magic on me. I make believe you're there; I talk with you and embrace the memories of our time spent together. Sometimes, I just go there to complete my studies for the next day.

Your parents want all of us to sit by their fireside, cook marshmallows, and listen to the stories you might have to tell us about Parris Island and Sgt. MedVecky. I just want to be charmed by the moment of our being together again. Everyone misses you very much, including Rubic. Your dad says he still sleeps by the front door every night. He is such a sweet and devoted dog.

As you know, I've started classes at Wellington and have decided my major field of study will be Secondary Education. I want to teach at C.R. someday. The professor I have for English Composition 101 is called Uncle Freddy by all the students. He calls us his little chirrups. I believe you had his class for English 101 too. I've written a couple of compositions so far

and have a B+ in one and an A in the other. Our next Essay is supposed to be about community improvement and how it will affect the public in general both pro and con.

All of my classes are first-year studies and so far I've been doing well. My test scores are all As and Bs. Since you've been away I have time to do what needs to be done. I'm either at the Mill Pond or in the library with all my energy being dedicated to study. Besides, I want to be on the Dean's List, graduate at the top of my class, and make you as proud of me as I am of you.

My most demanding class at the moment is Anatomy. We have to identify and learn all the bones, muscles, and systems of the human body. I'm going bananas with all the names and the correct spelling of everything. Professor Hughes takes points away for misspellings. You could have every question answered correctly but have it misspelled and he'll dock you five points per question.

I'm home in my room listening to a record of Elvis Presley as I write this letter to you. I must have 20 of his 45s. You know he's the only other man I love besides you. Now, don't be jealous. I just admire the way he sings all his love songs. Listening to the tender words in his love songs reminds me of you. I can't help it, but they make me cry. I miss you and can't wait until you return to me. Ever hear the new song by Dean Martin called "Return To Me"? I hear that and think of you. You are forever on my mind. I've loved you ever since we were children and I am yours forever. I anxiously await your arrival and pray every evening that time passes quickly and you return home safely to me.

All my love,

Rose Ann

DIARY ENTRY
Leaving Parris Island

Parting with the Marine Corps Recruit Depot Parris Island and saying farewell to Sgt. MedVecky was met with a great deal of approval on my part. Couldn't be happier as I've completed Basic Training USMC and have orders in my hand to the Naval Air Station Pensacola for flight training. I am to report on or about January 1, to The Marine Detachment Main Side for a pre-flight assignment to class 63-1 for my initial 12 weeks of ground school. The January 1 report date leaves me with the remainder of December for a trip home to see my family, friends, and Rose Ann. I've missed them all these past few months and I have the need to tell everyone what it has been like to bring to an end USMC Boot Camp. I now understand what it means when one Marine says to another Marine, "Semper Fi!"

A Private in the Corps makes a total of $78.00 per month as an E-1. Since I hadn't drawn any pay during recruit training I needed to stop by Dispersing and withdraw three months' back pay. After taxes I had $179 for a one-way trip home and a one-way ticket from Camden to my new duty station NAS Pensacola. Paydays are once a month, so I must be watchful of how and where I spend my money.

As I made my way to the main gate my thoughts ran back to that dark eventful night when I crossed under the Scarlet and Gold Archway to begin my recruit training. The memory of Sgt. MedVecky screaming at the top of his lungs during his sadistic and brutal introduction is still vivid in my mind. It had been my impression that sometime during recruit training that I would be murdered, castrated, or rendered mentally impotent by one of the Crazy Four.

On graduation day, immediately after all the pomp and circumstance, and just outside the main gate at P.I. there are always vans waiting to pick up newly graduated privates to give them a ride to the train station in Yamassee for a price. Along with a couple of other Marines from my platoon negotiations began with a driver for a point-to-point fair-price trip to the train station. With the price agreed, four of us threw our duffle bags into the trunk of the van and took our seats in the back. Thirty minutes later I stepped out at the station, dropped a five-dollar bill into the hand of the driver, and waited for him to give me my change. My percentage of the fare was all I wanted to pay. I knew he had to make a living, but I had to watch the pennies. I couldn't give away my money. I thanked him, he wished me luck, and I walked into the train station. Chills vibrated throughout my body thinking about that first gathering of my platoon that early morning hour of September 16, 1962. I felt comfort in knowing that Marine in the Smoky Bear Hat and I would never again cross paths. He was in the Infantry; I'm going into Aviation.

CHAPTER 9
HOMEWARD BOUND

According to Eddie's diary entries, his train ride to Pennsylvania and the return trip home was less nerve-racking than his southbound trip to Parris Island. He called his father after his graduation to give him a fair estimate of what time he would be arriving via trolley in Darby. Would he be able to pick him up at the station and save him the expense of an added bus ticket to Camden? If not, would he please leave the back door unlocked? His dad said he would pick him up on time as he was just as excited to see Eddie as Eddie was to see his father. They both missed the fireside talks as they huddled together to keep warm.

As the train pressed northward, the clickity clack of its wheels on the tracks were beginning to have a hypnotic effect on Eddie. He became absorbed with the countryside and fascinated by its peaceful appearance. Memories of home came rushing back all at once. Eddie had always been conscious of his environment, and watching the farmland pass by he thought of his best friend, Rubic. They had spent many hours together in the fields, river bottoms, and swamps, searching for rabbits. It was something he hadn't experienced in awhile and he made a promise that he would do just that while on leave. He missed his constant companion for two reasons: the hunt and the unconditional love the dog always gave

Eddie upon his return after a long separation. No one greeted him like that dog!

Returning his thoughts to the present, Eddie recalled the screaming, the senseless yelling, the unprovoked madness of training. He shook his head from side to side. So useless. That was history now. He was a temporary fugitive, better yet, a short-term escapee or an interim deserter. He was leaving the Marine Corps for three weeks and was happy to be away from the flies, the no-see-ums, the mosquitoes, and mostly Platoon 362's four mad Drill Instructors.

Revealing to Rose Ann's parents his affection, fondness, and devotion to her was the most important message he needed to relay to them before he made his return to the Corps and NAS Pensacola. Eddie intended to ask Rose Ann for her hand in marriage and to a greater extent wanted her parents to know how he felt about their daughter while he was at home on leave.

Remembering how apprehensive he was in asking Rose Ann to the back-to-school dance, how was he going to ask her father for her hand in marriage? He had never been so anxious or panicky of anything of this magnitude before. His hands shook as he tried to walk his mind through the steps it would take to actually ask for the girl's hand. Then again, he never asked anyone's father for their daughters hand in marriage. He had to set the stage so the event would be a pleasing and pleasant occasion. He also wanted them to know that one of the requirements of an applicant to be accepted into The Marine Aviation Cadet Program was that you had to be single and remain so throughout the training program. Upon graduating from advanced training, he would be commissioned a 2nd Lieutenant in the Marine Corps, pin on his Wings of Gold, and receive his designation as a Naval Aviator. With the closing stages of these three events he could marry anyone, any place, anytime, any race… just as long as it was a human being and of the opposite sex. Marine Corps policy regarding marriage has always been, "If the Corps wanted you to have a wife, they would have issued you one on the day of your enlistment." Eddie smiled at the thought.

At the moment, all he could do after asking her father for his blessing was ask Rose Ann for her hand in marriage, place on her finger an engagement ring, and the promise of marriage when he had completed the program. The Corps could care less if you married or continued to live a solitary life. As long as neither interfered with your obligation or commitment, being single or married was of little consequence to Headquarters Marine Corps. However, they really preferred you to be single and completely committed to the Eagle, Globe, and Anchor.

So much had changed since Eddie joined the Marine Corps. Yesterday was just a memory and only a photograph could bring back the moments they had captured in time. He sat there watching the landscape go by and would occasionally glance back inside to look at a picture of Rose Ann that he held tightly in his hand. It was a picture of her standing at water's edge there at the Wyoming's Mill Pond. That picture would have been lost forever if Eddie hadn't had his camera with him that warm summer afternoon.

He had been fishing for bass with Rose Ann watching him do what was so simple to him but so difficult for others. She was amazed that Eddie could catch so many fish with what she called the minimum of equipment. His fishing pole was about five feet long, made of bamboo; just a stick with about 10 feet of string tied to the very tip. He used a cork from a wine bottle as a bobber and the hooks he used were made from the ribs of a field mouse. The bait he used were earthworms dug up from his father's garden behind the house. It was amazing that he was successful in catching anything with the tools he had at his disposal.

When not fishing Eddie kept his prize earthworms in a Campbell's Soup can in his mother's refrigerator. The can was secured, covered by tin foil, encircled by a rubber band and hidden way in the back on the bottom shelf. It infuriated his mother to discover worms in her fridge. If she trashed one can of worms she trashed at least fifty over the years. It upset Eddie to discover his bait had been thrown away when he was just getting ready to jump on his bike and head out to the lake.

After what seemed like hours on the train Eddie arrived at Penn Central Station in Philly, made the transfer to the Darby Trolley, and 45 minutes later found his father waiting there on the platform just as he said he would be. They threw their arms around each other, tears swelled in their eyes, and they embraced each other as only a father and son could do after being apart for so long. Driving homeward they chatted about everything and nothing until Eddie fell asleep. He was exhausted mentally and physically. A trip home was just what he needed.

Pulling up to the house, Eddie could hear Rubic barking. The dog was waiting for him at the front door. When Rubic finally saw that one of the late arriving guests happened to be Eddie he went crazy. His days of faithful waiting at the front door had finally come to an end. He jumped around wildly, tail wagging, licking Eddie like a new- born pup. Now that his master was home, he wasn't about to let him out of his sight; not for a second. That night Rubic followed Eddie into his room, jumped up on his bed, and placed his head on Eddie's shoulder for the first night in many. The two old friends had a peaceful and uninterrupted night of rest, the first in a very long time.

Accustomed to rising early in the morning, Eddie's biological clock had him up around 6:00 a.m. He started planning the events of the day. His father had given him the use of the car for that weekend. David Willis, his father's shop manager, had agreed to re-arrange Eddie's father's schedule so he could have the weekend off to welcome Eddie home. David was a former Marine who had been with the First Marine Division, fought at Guadalcanal, was wounded and returned home minus his left leg from the knee down. Eddie was wearing the Eagle, Globe, and Anchor that he had earned at Parris Island, so David and Eddie were to be brothers forever. He was happy to do something for a brother Marine.

David was especially proud of Charlie's son, knowing he was a member of a minority group who had been fighting prejudices most of his life. Somehow he had found a way to be accepted into an elite pilot program in the Marine Corps. Selected from the enlisted ranks into the officer corps is an enormous achievement for anyone, especially as an alternative applicant, an American Indian. He was an Apache Indian, and the Corps wanted him in the MarCad Program for that undeniable reason. At least that was what David assumed. Recalling his time in the Corps, David knew the road ahead for him would be a challenging one. Gifts in the Corps are earned and not given.

CHAPTER 10
SWEET ROSE ANN

Eddie's diary lead me deeper and deeper into his mindset over time. It began to feel like I was this young man in love, working hard to get ahead in the Marines, struggling against prejudice. I found myself thinking about his story even when I wasn't reading the entries. I was becoming Eddie's friend and fan.

According to his notes about his return home, it was obvious that all Eddie wanted to do was phone Rose Ann and let her know he finally arrived home. He couldn't wait to see her. Second, he wanted to arrange that traditional conversation with her father, and if he received the man's blessing, he would purchase an engagement ring at Todd's Jewelry in downtown Dover. However, Eddie had to put the fun part off for a few more hours. He had to see Rose Ann's father first.

Eddie called Rose Ann. It was a quick call. She had classes all morning… had to rush or she'd be late. They agreed to meet in front of the Fine Arts Building around 1 o'clock that afternoon. Rose Ann then handed her father the phone. Eddie wanted to say hello to the man. What he really wanted to do was talk to her father in the morning and meet Rose Ann later that afternoon.

It was working out just as he had planned. The father would meet with him around 10:00 a.m. to talk about "significant events" in his and hopefully Rose Ann's life. Confident that her father would figure out the subject matter or theme of their would-be exchange, Eddie anticipated his blessing and expected him to let it go at that. The father had his own agenda. Eddie was to go through the excruciating ritual dreaded by all bachelors, the acceptance and agonizing blessing of his future father-in-law. There would be no easy path.

About an hour later, at the home where Rose Ann had grown up and where she continued to reside, Eddie asked her father for her hand in marriage. He just had to find him first. Rose Ann's dad was in the barn, sitting on a short three-legged stool, milking Clara, his prize Jersey cow. This was not what Eddie had imagined.

As Eddie entered the barn, Rose Ann's father looked up at him.

"Pull a bale of hay from the adjacent stall there and bring it over here," said the girl's father. "You can use it as a seat."

Maybe that would be good. At least that way they would have better eye contact as they carried on with their conversation and the man could continue his milking.

Eddie began his prepared speech. "I love your daughter. She means everything to me. I've loved her since we were kids. You know that. It's no secret. I want her to be my wife. As an officer and pilot, I will make enough money to give her the life she deserves. I'm here to ask for your daughter's hand. I want your permission, Sir."

Rose Ann's father stopped milking Clara. He looked Eddie straight in the eye. Eddie thought the man was weighing out whether to punch him in the face or welcome him into the family. It could go either way. The man stuck out his hand for Eddie to take and told him he looked good in Marine Green. He said that he'd be honored to have Eddie as a son-in-law. To Eddie, this was the second best thing that happened to him since joining the Corps. Now he just needed Rose Ann to agree to marry him.

It would be an engagement of approximately eighteen months. The extended engagement would give Rose Ann adequate time to complete two years of studies, make arrangements to transfer all her earned credits to a university close to Eddie's next duty station, and then begin the next chapter in their lives. Eddie made a pledge to her father that he would see to it that she completed her work toward her lifelong desire of becoming a teacher. It was Rose Ann's passion to touch as many people as she could through teaching.

Eddie stood at the front of the Fine Arts Building at exactly 1:00 p.m. He told her that they were just having lunch together. She had no idea about the rest of his plan. It was there, in front of about a half a dozen of Rose Ann's classmates that Eddie knelt down. On bended knee, he asked Rose Ann for her hand in marriage.

Telling her that he had met with her father just a few hours earlier and

that he had received the man's blessing, he wanted to know if she loved him enough to become Mrs. Blizzard and be his wife forever. Rose Ann didn't have to be asked twice. She threw her arms around Eddie's neck and kissed him. Of course the answer was YES.

The onlookers broke into applause. It was like a party, with congratulations flung from everyone to the happy couple. It was a moment to remember. Eddie and Rose Ann were suddenly surrounded by her classmates. Eddie had one last thing to do before taking his girl to lunch. It was time to make a stop at Todd's Jewelry and let Rose Ann choose an engagement ring. Eddie's father had given him $200.00 as an engagement gift to use toward a ring if she accepted. It would be well spent.

Eddie had the rest of his leave time to adjust to the idea of marriage and the future. He would serve his country and take care of his wife. He liked that idea. The couple knew they were going to spend the rest of their lives together, but they also knew that because Eddie signed a contract with the Corps that he would be obligated first to serving the Corps and Country. These would always come first, at least for the next five years. While in training the couple could only see each other during holidays or periods where Eddie was ending one phase of training and beginning another. Between phases he may get to leave and return home for short periods of time. Maybe Eddie could save up enough of his cadet pay to send to Rose Ann, so she could come see him between semesters or during certain holidays. She had school and studies, too, but even with these scheduling complications the two vowed to make it work.

DIARY ENTRY
January 1, 1963

Today is New Year's Day and a Tuesday. I just finished checking in at the Marine Detachment NAS Pensacola. The OD was a 1st Lieutenant by the name of McGovern, a Naval Aviator assigned to administrative work and office duty over the holiday period. I suspect that the remaining office personnel are off through the New Year's holiday. Only people working in the office area are 1st Lt. McGovern and a Marine, PFC Gardner. I presume Gardner was on the duty roster Friday to Tuesday evening to assist in typing orders, emergency leaves, and the like. While checking in I heard a TV from the adjacent room. I could hear a football game. The staff were probably watching it when they could. I heard the USC/Ohio State commentary and play-by-play in the background.

Beginning to learn that rank has its privileges. McGovern, my guess, was the lowest-ranking officer in S-1 at the MATD. For that reason, he was assigned O.D. over the holidays. PFC Gardner was his assistant. Beginning to learn the lower your rank the more meaningless tasks you'll be assigned over weekends and holidays. Got to get used to it as I am now somewhere between an enlisted man and an officer. PFC Gardner seemed less than happy that I was interrupting his TV time.

I turned over my records, my orders from HQ Marine Corps assigning me to Flight Training. I received instructions on where to go and to whom to report. I was then directed to the Pre-Flight Building where

both NavCads and MarCads check-in for their initial indoctrination and assignment.

There were approximately 10 other Cadets milling around, wondering what was going to happen next, when I checked into the Indoctrination Building. A big guy about six feet tall and skinny as a rail was laughing and carrying on like a little kid. I wondered if he was going to make it through the program before being disciplined out. Surprisingly, he was an articulate, outgoing, southern boy from Mississippi named Ken Owen. I liked him already as he could bring a smile to anyone's face with very little effort.

Owen told everyone to guard their hair. Had an Indian coming on-board. "Pass the word, we need someone on watch throughout the night. Gotta make sure we're safe when the lights go out." Everyone laughed and immediately started to introduce themselves to me. Tagged me with the nickname "Chief."

I assured them I wasn't a chief. Just a violent warrior and the great grandson of Geronimo, War Chief of the Chiricahuas Apache. I wasn't just an ordinary Indian. I was as mean as a junkyard dog, possessed an uncompromising temper, and my weapon of choice was the knife. Without more ado, Owen backed off. It looked like he might be wondering if he had overstepped the boundary of friendship. Seeing me smile, he knew everything was going to be okay. My new classmates gathered around me and decided my call sign when flying should be "Geronimo."

Before long there were 25 cadets in the squad bay awaiting orders. Of those, 18 were NavCads; the remainder MarCads. Of the seven MarCads, two were former enlisted Marines; one from Parris Island, me, and a Corporal who had been a member of a helicopter squadron attached to Marine Corps Air Station, Santa Ana, California, FMF. If both of us complete the program and receive our commissions, we'll be known as Mustangs, a name given to Marines transitioning from the enlisted ranks to the Officer Corps.

If the enlisted personnel in your outfit knew you were a Mustang they'd work their heart out for you. Their fellow junior officers passed judgment on them and thought them uncouth, vulgar, foul-mouthed, unpolished, and bad mannered. Love/hate relationship. The Marine Corps accepted them throughout the lower ranks – 2nd Lieutenant/1st Lieutenant/ Captain – and needed their aggressive no-nonsense approach to duty. They would be given a task and you can bet the farm it will be finished on schedule. They blindly attacked their duty with passion with minimum amounts of discord. Senior officers didn't particularly care for Mustangs either. If at all possible they assign these renegades to duties that coincide with military functions, squadron events, or any social gatherings. Coming from the enlisted ranks as a Private and getting a commission as a Lieutenant will make me a Mustang. I'll look forward to working with the men.

Indoctrination Battalion

Just as in boot camp there was about to be an introduction made by what appeared to be another spiffy Marine Drill Instructor. He was short, about five foot six, built like a Mack truck. Not a wrinkle in his uniform, shoes that had a surface shine like glass, and three rows of ribbons over his left breast pocket. A clone of Sgt. MedVecky in dress, but this man's intro was the complete opposite. He started by saying, "Gentleman, my name is Staff Sgt. Shane. When you address me you will call me Sgt. Shane. When I address you, I will call you Mister So and So or whatever your last name happens to be. Example: Mr. Kelly. You will be with me for the next five days and periodically over the next 12 weeks for all of your military training." Not a cuss word escaped his lips.

"On my request, please pick up all your personal belongings and exit this building via the door you entered. On the sidewalk in front of this building you will find painted footprints. Find yourself any pair of footprints and stand on them. Have I made my instructions clear?"

We all replied in unison, "Yes Sgt. Shane."

"Gentleman, gather up your gear and exit the building."

With everyone outside and with each of us on a spot, we appeared to be in a platoon formation. Sgt. Shane directed us to face or turn in place to our left and follow him on his command. He was taking us to the barracks where we would live and study for the remainder of our pre-

flight training.

Moving like a herd of cattle rather than a well-trained military unit – like a mob without a leader – we arrived at our permanent living quarters. Sgt. Shane began his brief on what was going to happen as soon as we entered the building.

"Class 63-1, get in single file. One by one, step in front of the desk in the foyer, and I will assign you a room along with a roommate. In your assigned room you will find two desks, two racks, and two double lockers – one for each of you assigned to that room. You will be given a lock, and all your valuables along with you uniforms will be stored in this locker. Your locker will be secured and locked at all times, except when you open it to retrieve clothes, uniforms, books, money, whatever. You will never, I repeat, never leave your locker open whenever you are not in your room. Let me forewarn you, and I must. The Marine Corps and the Navy dislike thieves. If you steal anything from anyone, when you are caught, and you will be, you will be given a Court Martial. You will be purged or dishonorably discharged from the Navy or the Marine Corps, and good riddance to you. I am sorry I had to address such an issue, but it is in the directives that it be mentioned to all incoming personnel. Do you understand?"

We all said at once, "Yes, Sir!"

"No! It's yes, Sgt. Shane. Let it never be mentioned again." With that he turned and walked away.

January 2, 1963

The remainder of yesterday was spent getting our room assignments along with each of us being assigned a roommate. My roommate is a NavCad by the name Robert O'Malley, an Irish kid from Long Island. We got to talking. He had attended a two-year school in Morrisville, New York... Morrisville Jr. College. Graduated with a pre- engineering degree in Civil Engineering. Wanted to go transfer to MIT, but wasn't accepted, so he decided to enter the NavCad Program.

O'Malley is a little guy. Had blond hair, weighed about 130 pounds at best. Definitely not an athlete; probably a real scholar. Strangest thing about him is that he has one blue eye one gray eye. I assumed he had excellent vision in both eyes or he wouldn't be in the program. It felt weird not knowing which eye to look into while we carried on a conversation. Struggled with it and finally convinced myself it would do more harm to question him, so I decided to let it go. Already have a feeling about the guys in the Class of 63-1; they'll probably give him the call sign "Two Eyes."

All of us spent the morning at the barbershop. I knew what was com- ing as it had happened once before at Parris Island. Twice in the past four months I've involuntarily had my head shaved. Takes three months before it will be manageable enough to be seen in public. The irony of it all was the Department of the Navy was about to charge me 25 cents to look like a fool. Shortly after haircuts we were fitted for uniforms. Picked up basic shirts, trousers, shoes, and emblems. Items that made us look somewhat like a military unit until we received our final issue.

After uniform fitting/sizing we went to a classroom where a Marine Captain told us to take a seat, addressed, and answered what had been on all our minds for the past few hours. He started by telling us we were to be tested in math within the hour. The results of the test would determine whether we needed a refresher course in the subject before entering the regular 12-week pre-flight course. Refresher courses are two weeks in length. Seventy is a passing score. After two weeks of extra instruction, if you fail to meet a minimum score of 70 on the final exam, you will be asked to leave the program, and will be transferred to a new assignment in the Navy or Marine Corps.

We were given instructions. "You are on the honor system. There will be no cheating and you will turn in all classmates who are known to you that have cheated. If it is found out that you do not turn in a cheater and it is discovered by a superior that you covered for that cheater, you will both be asked to leave the program. There is no room in the Officer Corps for a cheater. Do you all understand?" We all agreed that we did.

The instructor continued. "Along with your military and classroom requirements we have a discipline/demerit system. For each infraction, misconduct, or deficiency that you receive from Upper class Cadet Officers, Classroom Instructors, or your Military Training Instructor, you can be given from five to 15 demerits. For every five demerits you receive, you will spend one hour on the parade field where you will march the infraction off. Demerits will be marched off on the weekends. You are allowed a total of 60 demerits while in your pre-flight phase of training. Exceed that and you will be asked to leave the program for cause. Examples of infractions are bunks not made properly, late for formation, and improper dress or dirty uniform. Serious infractions will be dealt with by the Academic Director or me, since I am your Class Officer."

Three hours later Captain Graves informed the class that seven members of Class 63-1 had failed the math test. I had failed with an incoming score of 16. I knew when I learned of my failing grade that I had a long row to hoe to make it through the program. I vowed to get a better grade on the final.

CHAPTER 11
TESTING BEGINS

Eddie's first test at the Training Command and the results were not exactly what he had expected. Math wasn't his strong suit, but he figured on doing a bit better than a 16. Captain Graves informed him that he had received a score of 16 on the math exam and that he had his doubts that he would be successful in achieving a 70% even with the extra two weeks of tutoring. He was at the bottom of the class, the lowest of the low, and no cadet had ever received a score as tainted as his to go on to passing the final after the refresher course. It was going to be virtually impossible for him to pass, according to Graves, who openly wondered how Eddie had ever been accepted into the program.

All Eddie could think about was his failure and lack of achievement in academics while at C.R. and Wellington. Football had been his master, and now it was his retribution and punishment. He was embarrassed to stand in front of Captain Graves and explain the events that brought him to this crater of failure. He asked Captain Graves if he would be his mentor and give special tutoring after class in the evening, anytime, anywhere. Unfortunately, he would have to find someone in his class to act as his aide and bring to an end the course in the fixed time frame allotted to all cadets. The math course began with Algebra 1 and ended with Trigonometry, which had to be successfully completed or Eddie was going back to the Fleet Marine Force as a Private. His first thought was Owen. Was he in the refresher course? He was indeed, and he offered to help Eddie as much as he could.

For the next two weeks Eddie studied math from 0800 to 1600 in the classroom and from 1800 to 2200 (Lights Out) with Ken Owen in the cadet barracks. Friday morning came; with it came the two-hour final exam. Eddie failed with a score of 68. Eddie was the only one to fail the final, and according to his diary he was agonizing over how to inform Rose Ann, his parents, and friends back home. He just knew he was about to be dropped from the program before it really began.

Captain Graves dismissed the remainder of Class 63-1 and released them from any duties for the rest of the day. He requested Eddie to re-main seated as he needed to talk to him. Eddie thought… here it comes. Unexpectedly, Captain Graves told Eddie he would stand beside him in the Academic Directors Office and ask for a waiver of academic failure on his behalf.

Captain Graves told the A.D., Commander Woodson, that Eddie had made remarkable progress in improving his original scores of 16 to 68 in such a short time, and that he was convinced that Eddie would be successful if given an additional week of study. He felt it would be an in-justice to Cadet Blizzard and to the Marine Corps to discharge this cadet from the program. The Marine Corps needed people like Eddie as future officers in aviation. Captain Graves offered his personal time as a tutor to

Eddie in the classroom environment if the A.D. would waive his failure status.

Here was a Captain in the USMC, an officer that knew Eddie only as a student in his classroom, standing beside him in front of Commander Woodson's desk, asking his superior to give Cadet Blizzard something that was highly irregular, out of the ordinary, and certainly unconventional as a military request.

A Marine in harm's way will always have his call countered by his brothers in arms without hesitation. The Marine motto "Semper Fidelis" surfaced before Eddie's eyes via Captain Graves. His commitment, loyalty, and dedication was an outreach of one Marine to another. He was asking for nothing more in return than a "Semper Fi" and a handshake. Done deal.

Commander Woodson looked up from his desk, gave Eddie the one additional week, and told him he didn't want to see him in his office again. He added that if Eddie failed next time that he would be transferred back to Fleet Marine Force, Camp LeJeune, North Carolina, for Infantry training. Infantry training? That was not on Eddie's to-do list. He would pass that test come hell or high water.

The original class 63-1 that had passed all the entry tests moved forward in their studies. Those who were held back and passed the math after the two weeks of extra study joined Class 63-2. Eddie passed the math after the third week of additional instruction and would join Class

63-3. New classes begin every other week, which left Eddie a week of waiting for 63-3. In the meantime he moved out of his original quarters and into new quarters. Things were looking up.

Over the next 12 weeks Eddie took and passed Math, Physics, Aerodynamics, Meteorology, Navigation, Aviation Rules and Regulations, Survival Tactics, Swimming, Dilbert Dunker (escape from aircraft cockpit under water), Aviation Physiology, Naval and Marine Corps History, Aircraft Engines and Systems, and last but not least, he passed Military Instruction, Conduct and Performance.

Successfully completing the pre-flight curriculum Eddie would now be transferred to NAS Saufley Field for primary flight training in the T-34B Mentor, a two-place, tandem, low-wing, single-engine aircraft. Eddie was thrilled.

DIARY ENTRY
April 21, 1963

The past week (Easter) has been a week of limbo. My Class of 63-3 completed the prescribed academics at NAS Pensacola and has transferred from Mainside to the cadet barracks here at AAS Saufley Field. John McCants and Carl Walton have been asked to leave the program for academic reasons. Twenty-three cadets remaining in our class. Have been assigned a room with a cadet from Willow Grove, Pennsylvania. Cadet Powers, NavCad, two years at the University of Pennsylvania. Medium-size guy, more than 200 pounds. Looks like a slob and acts like a slob. Personal hygiene is suspect. Twelve weeks in my class and really never got to know him. Don't care to either.

According to Cadet Powers, he majored in business at Penn, which required too much effort on his part so he decided to apply for and was accepted into the Cadet Program. (Like this program is going to be any easier.) Told me he had about 50 hours of flight time in Cessna's before coming to Pensacola. Didn't plan to tell his instructor about the flight time.

Not knowing Powers had a Private Pilots License would give the instructor the mindset that he was an outstanding student when basically he would be an average student. Powers was shooting the system. He had pre-planned to benefit by having flight time and not providing that information to his instructor. He knew flight grades were given to a student by his instructor by the way the cadet carried out the individual maneuvers required in the syllabus. Prior flight time would definitely aide him in his deception.

Grades were either above average, average, or below average. If the instructor ascertained that a student was dangerous to himself or others, he would recommend that student be dropped from the program. Powers' background in aviation certainly would be beneficial to him in any of the maneuvers he had to perform for his instructor.

Only those achieving the highest grades were chosen for Jets (fighter or attack aircraft training). Pipeline vacancies in transports and helicopters were to be filled by individual requests or assignments from the Training Command depending upon the number of openings in each category. Powers knew all the ins and outs before arriving at Pensacola.

What I drew from my chitchat with Cadet Powers was that he has a serious character flaw. He is a con artist and cheat. I gave him an option. "Tell your instructor about your flight time or I will. We have an honor system. It is my duty and responsibility to bring any infraction considered to be cheating to the attention of my superiors and I will."

Powers was stunned! I was not going to let him use deception in gaining a billet into jets. He was going to earn it just like the rest of us. He should be dropped from the program for intent to defraud. Not officer material.

Collecting my thoughts, I left the room, went to the Officer in Charge, and requested a room change. Powers watched me enter his office. The substance of my discussion with the OIC was never disclosed to Cadet Powers, but a lesson in integrity, truthfulness, and principle was learned that day. Not knowing what I had to say to the OIC would force him to admit his indiscretion and act accordingly. His character needed a major modification. I intended to help him along.

Denied a room change. OIC said I had to learn to achieve any mission put before me either working with someone I liked or someone I found intolerable. Powers name never came up in his office other than the fact that I wanted a room change. Accepted the outcome. Didn't change the fact my roommate was still an overweight cheater who had quit school and was now attempting to shoot the system. Will he make it through the program? Will he be discharged from the program for lying, cheating, or lack of performance? Time will tell. Before his flight status or training began I found out that he told his instructor about his previous flight time. Needless to say, I was then relieved of my responsibility to inform my superiors of his character flaws. Good.

CHAPTER 12
HISTORY LESSON: U. S. NAVAL AUXILIARY AIR STATION SAUFLEY FIELD, PENSACOLA, FLORIDA

NAS Saufley Fields origin began in 1939 with the Department of the Navy's purchase of approximately 900 acres west of Pensacola, Florida. Construction on the airfield began almost immediately in August 1939 and was completed by August 1940. The field was named after Lieutenant Junior Grade Richard C. Saufley, Naval Aviator #14 who was killed in a training exercise on June 9, 1916.

The purchase of the property was from an elderly couple in their 80s who were living on the property at the time of contract. In the contract they included a provision that embraced the couple's right to live out the remainder of their lives in their home on what was soon to become military property.

Personnel on the base grew to know the couple and treated them with reverence. As time passed the Sailors and Marines provided the couple with security, medical care, food, and handyman service whenever needed. The gentleman passed away in 1943; the wife in 1948.

The field has three runways, a North/South (18/36) located on the far eastern part of the base, and two runways constructed in the shape of an X: Northeast/Southwest (04/22), and Northwest/Southeast (32/14). The VT-1 hanger is located on the southeast corner. On the southwest corner the VT-5 hanger is used for T-28 Bs and Cs Carrier Qualification Students. Instructor Indoctrination Training is conducted in the T-34, and T-28 programs are also carried out in these buildings.

The hanger used for VT-1 is divided into four quarters. Three are used for Navy personnel, and the fourth is a Marine Section called Flight 18. Eddie has been assigned to Flight 18, the Marine section. Entering the Ready Room of Flight 18 you see that the room is divided into two parts; a section for the students and a private section for the instructors. Each Ready Room has adequate numbers of lockers to accommodate the students and the instructors for their flight gear. The lockers hold the necessary equipment needed by each individual to carry out the flights, such as helmets, flight suit, clip boards, study material, and other issued and necessary paraphernalia. There are also a number of tables and chairs throughout the room that are used by the students for various reasons. Instructors use these tables as briefing and debriefing stations for their students. Students are not allowed in the instructor area unless invited.

The VT-1 syllabus is the first coursework aviators go through and is commonly called Pre-Solo. PS 1-12 is dual with an instructor, and P13 is your first solo flight. With the initial phase of training complete the final phase of training at VT-1 is called Precision (P1-10). The flights are primarily an introduction to aerobatics with the student learning the barrel roll, loops, Cuban eights, spins, and figure eights. Five flights dual and five flights solo.

In the student area of the Ready Room a large Flight Board, much like a chalkboard, with instructors' names in red sprawls across the entirety of the back wall. Beneath each instructor's name in a descending column and numbered one through five are all the students assigned to each instructor. The student names are in blue. Beside each of the students' names in orange is the current flight number. This is their next training flight. The board advises the instructor what flight is planned for his student on which specific day. It could be a PS flight or a PCN flight, depending how far along the student is in the program.

Just in front of the scheduling board sits the Operations Officer's desk. The Ops Officer keeps the board up to date as the instructors go in and out of the ready room, completing their flights for the day. He marks each student's flight as complete, incomplete, warm-up, or unsatisfactory from informational reports received from individual instructors.

If a student hasn't flown in more than five days he is granted a warm-up flight (WUF). The reason for delay can be caused by weather, illness, or emergency leave. If the warm-up flight is taken, completed and acceptable to the instructor, the student will be advanced to his next scheduled flight. If in the instructor's opinion the flight is not equal to or better than the past performance the student can use this flight as a warm-up. A warm-up is a warm-up. You cannot get a down. You can be advanced but not given an unsatisfactory for proficiency. That's a "freebie."

Students who receive an unsatisfactory from an instructor will be given a new instructor (a personality conflict could be the cause for failure). The student will be given two extra warm-ups and a recheck. If his progress is graded unsatisfactory after the additional extra flights and a recheck, the new instructor will recommend the student be dropped from the program. At this point, the student is given what is called a Speedy Board. This board determines whether the student is to be given additional flight time or removed and reassigned to the Navy or Marine Corps and the needs of their service.

More often than not the board will give the student two additional flights, a recheck, and re-evaluation. As a rule, if a student returns to the Speedy Board a second time he will be dropped from the program. Seldom or almost never will the Chief of Naval Air Training, Vice Admiral Robert A. Ranson, intervene on behalf of a student. The students' personal safety and that of others is the primary reason for the Admiral stepping aside and being unapproachable. That's how it is. No questions asked.

DIARY ENTRY
April 22, 1963

0800 Monday Morning began with orientation. Discovered that along with the necessary subjects pertaining to the T34B, we have courses in Aviation Rules, Regulations, Navigation, Morse code, and Blinker. Beginning tomorrow morning at 0800 we will have three one-hour courses per day for a week on various subjects on the aircraft. Power Plant (engine), Hydraulics, Flight Controls, and Aircraft Specifications (electronics, dimensions, weights, speeds). Afternoons are gifted to us to use as study periods and we are free of all obligations. Morse Code and Blinker start tonight at 1800 immediately after chow.

Code/Blinker classes are on Monday, Wednesday, and Friday evenings. Only requirement made for all students were to pass the final on Code and Blinker prior to being transferred to T-28 Trojans at VT-2 Whiting Field, Milton, Florida, or T2J Buckeyes at VT-7 NAS Meridian, Mississippi, for those going into jets.

Tuesday and Thursday evenings (1800) we have the Mock-Up C/P (cockpit) time; six-hour requirement. Teamed up with another student. Have to demonstrate by pointing to the instruments on the instrument panel everything from airspeed indicator to altimeter, including throttle quadrant, trim tabs, flap controls, circuit breakers and anything that moves or is stationary in the C/P. As a final exam I must point to and tell the instructor what and where everything is located BLINDFOLDED. This has to be completed and passed before being assigned to a flight instructor. It's all a little stressful and a whole lot overwhelming, but I will do it, and I will pass!

Wrote Rose Ann a letter and a short note to Mom and Dad. Told them I have very little free time as I'm busy with ground school during the day, followed by Code, Blinker, and late study well into the night. They should not expect lengthy letters from me. I hope they aren't too disappointed.

CHAPTER 13
WINGS OF AN EAGLE

Eddie breezed through academics. In fact, he finished with a GPA of 3.5 and passed the Code and Blinker. He was assigned an instructor and though he had a little trouble with the Blinker he finally passed. He was told to report to Flight 18, seek out his instructor, get a locker assignment from the Duty Officer, and draw his flight gear.

Entering Flight 18 Eddie looked up and down the flight board. He finally found his name in blue with the PS-1 adjacent to it. Above his name were the names of the additional students assigned to his instructor. To the right of their names in bold print was their next scheduled flight. Most were in PCN stage. Eddie was the instructor's only new student.

Eddie was assigned Captain James Brenner, USMC, a regular officer with one deployment to Viet Nam. Most Americans didn't know that US Forces at that time were in Viet Nam actively engaged with the enemy. In April of 1962 Captain Brenner had deployed to Da Nang as a member of HMM 366, a UH34D helicopter squadron participating in Operation Shufly. He had been a 7335 (helicopter pilot) who had earned the Silver Star, Distinguished Flying Cross, and Purple Heart all in the time span of six months. Remarkable military achievement in such a short time.

Everyone in the squadron knew of Captain Brenner and his reputation. Eddie was lucky to have drawn him as his instructor. He was going to be proud and honored just to walk one step behind and one step to the left of him anywhere he walked.

Learning the physical description of Captain Brenner from the Duty Officer he recognized the man immediately. He and one of his students had just completed a flight and were walking in from the flight line. They sat down at one of the debriefing tables and were discussing the progress his student had made in certain maneuvers, thrashing out areas that needed improvement.

Capt. Brenner was the smallest person in Flight 18. Just five feet six inches tall, he looked malnourished at about 120 pounds. His black hair and a thin Errol Flinn mustache made him stand out. Plus, he walked with a slight limp in his left leg. Before reporting to Pensacola Brenner had spent three months at the Naval Hospital in Bethesda, Maryland, rehabilitating from wounds received while carrying out a rescue mission. Scuttlebutt had it that a Vietnamese recon team with two KIAs and three WIAs was surrounded, holding out on top of a hill. They were about to be overrun and desperately needed to be evacuated from their location in the Quang Ngai area. Quang Ngai was a Viet Minh stronghold southwest of Da Nang. Brenner and his crew had answered their call and had paid the price.

Meeting for the first time, Brenner asked if Eddie was an American Indian and where he made his home. They discussed Eddie's heritage, which was refreshing, because the instructor seemed genuinely interested. Their conversation was a question-and-answer period with Captain Brenner doing his best to orchestrate a comfortable setting between he and Eddie, who became more at ease the longer he and Captain Brenner talked. By the end of the conversation Eddie knew what Brenner expected of him as his student.

Captain Brenner told him that all his students were allowed an exemption of one scheduled flight, on any given day, for any reason. The students called it "pardon for the day." All they had to do was tell Captain Brenner they wanted the day off and it was so. Most of his students seldom took advantage of this generous proposal. It was up to Eddie to decide whether he would accept Captain Brenner's proposition in the future. Maybe someday he would need that day off for one reason or another. Eddie's self confidence grew the more he spoke with his mentor and was ecstatic to be setting in motion his aviation career.

DIARY ENTRY
April 28

Completed the Cockpit Box Check as it is called; passed with little difficulty. Cadet Pierce, a NavCad friend of mine, and I have spent endless hours pointing out each and every gage, switch, and knob to each other. We had zero trouble finishing the blindfold test. I knew I could do it! I wish I could share this right now with my father. I know he would be very proud. So would Rose Ann.

I'm now studying the procedures for PS-1. Each flight from PS-1 to PS-12 has certain items the instructor must introduce along with random review items from previous flights. Review procedures can be anything from a spin to a wing over as long as they are in the syllabus and have been previously introduced.

PS-1 is a mouthful! I must know the procedure for the following: complete a Pre flight or airworthiness of the aircraft. Must know engine start, taxi, take off, slow flight, introduction into the traffic pattern, and landing procedures. PS1 usually lasts about an hour and thirty minutes. A lot of material for a student to learn prior to his first flight.

Spent the morning drawing the following flight gear: boots, survival knife, leather gloves, clipboard, flight suit, helmet, and microphone. Talk about anticipation! My life is filled with unbelievable enthusiasm. Met and talked with my flight instructor. Enjoyed our first meeting and introduction. Can't wait to get on with my training!!

CHAPTER 14
NAS SAUFLY

Eddie's PS-1 was everything he expected it to be. Captain Brenner introduced him to the aircraft in the sequence he expected. It was a flight in which his instructor had an abundance of items to introduce. He had to familiarize Eddie with the geographical boundaries in the southern section of the training area. He pointed out four auxiliary airfields that he would use for practice landings and to acquaint Eddie with them as the western and southern boundaries of the training area. He advised Eddie of the northern area by using other visual aids on the grounds, such as towers, highways and country roads. The captain made it clear that Eddie was not to go beyond these borders for safety reasons. That way, in the event Eddie had an emergency that would require him to land in a farmer's field, rescue crews would know in what area to search.

These airfields were also to be used for practicing the Standard Navy Break (entrance to a naval field) at 1,000 feet. Santa Rosa, Summerdale, Foley, and Fairhope along the southern and western sections were points that marked the beginning of restricted areas. Flights could not be flown beyond these geographical landmarks. No side trips to Mobile, Baton Rouge, or New Orleans, and definitely no flights over Pensacola Bay, the gulf, or Mobile Bay. Learning his way around the area, staying out of the commercial airway corridor to the north, and finding his way home to Saufley were just a few of the things Eddie had to remember for PS-1.

Throughout the flight Captain Brenner showed Eddie various attitudes of the aircraft's nose for normal cruise, slow flight or dirty flight, with gear and flaps extended. Eddie performed several maneuvers, performing them from average to above average performance. Trimming the aircraft, using the trim tabs for the rudder, aileron, and stabilizer, was the hardest for Eddie. For a full five minutes he had to hold the aircraft completely out of trim in the normal cruise attitude. When Captain Brenner finally said, "Trim out the pressures using the trim tabs," Eddie was more than willing. He certainly wouldn't need another five-minute demo to keep the aircraft in trim. Attempting to trim the aircraft was never an issue again.

"Trim, trim, trim" was persistently called out during each and every maneuver thereafter. Captain Brenner frequently made Eddie place his hands on top of his helmet to see if the a/c was in trim or if Eddie was holding all the pressures. The captain tried to convey to Eddie that it is more fun to fly an a/c when it's in trim and certainly a lot easier. For the next 11 flights Eddie proved to be an above average student with an all-consuming desire to enter the jet syllabus.

DIARY ENTRY
May 15, 1963

Today marked my first big step in becoming a Naval Aviator. I successfully completed my P12 check ride. A Navy Lieutenant (Hall) from the adjoining training section out of flight 16 was assigned to me as my check airman. Throughout the check ride, Lt. Hall made me jump through all the hoops, sound all the bells and whistles, and complete successfully all the required procedures before entering the landing pattern at Foley Auxiliary for three touch-and-go landings. While on the third approach for a landing, Lt. Hall told me over the intercom to make it a full stop. Upon landing and rolling out he told me to exit the runway, taxi to the take off area in the vicinity of the Runway Duty Officer (RDO), and then stop. Making the stop near Paddles, Lt. Hall told me to set the parking brake, open my canopy, and await further instructions. All of a sudden, he was out of the rear cockpit, kneeling on the wing next to me, asking if I was ready to solo. Talk about a bolt out of the blue or lightning striking, all I could say was, "If you get off the wing, Sir, I'll be on my way." He looked surprised. What he didn't know is that I was just as surprised as I hadn't planned on saying that, but I was anxious to solo. Couldn't wait another minute!

He ordered me to do one touch-and-go, one full-stop landing, and return to the very spot I'd started from to retrieve him. If I left him at Foley and flew back to Saufley without him he'd see to it I went to Leavenworth for a minimum of five years.

Tapping me on top of the helmet, he jumped off the wing and saluted. Once he was clear of the aircraft and standing next to the RDO, I closed the canopy on my aircraft and scanned the approach area to make sure I wasn't interfering with any arriving aircraft. Taxiing onto the runway I positioned myself on the centerline, completed the takeoff checklist, released the brakes, added power, and raced down the runway. Within a few seconds I was airborne. I remember Captain Brenner saying to me, "Just fly the aircraft; have fun." So I did.

Landmark moment in Marine Cadet Edward P. Blizzard's life!! Got an up on my check ride and went solo!

Officers of 374 awaiting transport to MCAS Okinawa. C130 out of Marine Corp Air Station, El Toro. January 25, 1965.

Note the prices of food for visiting officers and non-military personnel. Marine's eat for free!

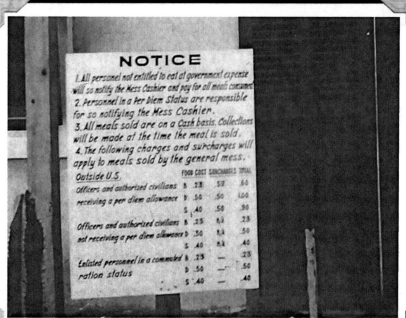

Pilots gambled, drank and had fun behind these doors, no weapons allowed.
Ordering drinks using "dirty" words was a frequent game!

All the aircraft logs were kept here. It's also where all maintenance
paperwork was completed.

Da Nang Airfield still under construction in the early 60s. Note the up-to-date "tower"!

Pilot Ready Room and maintenence shack.

Happy to have returned home from their last mission.

Staging area Operation Armageddon early morning all hands in aircraft awaiting turnup signal.

Staging area at Chu Lai Operation Backwash
Drop Zone, LZ Harbor, south side of the Tra Bong River.

Pilots were killed during Operation Backwash. Aircraft recovered used for spare parts.

Captured weapons from earlier missions.

Pilots writing their after-action reports.

Wounded men rescued by Marines just outside Chu Lai. These men crashed five miles east of Hill 415 during Operation Backwash, lucky to be alive!

CHAPTER 15
NAS WHITING

That was the shortest entry in Eddie's diary, but I can see why. What more was there to say? He was making his dream to become a pilot come true. According to the notes in his diary at that time, Eddie finished up his PCN 1-10 uneventfully and awaited his orders. He said that he hoped he would be transferred to Meridian and the T2J Buckeye to fly jets. His overall grades in flight and ground school came to a 3.28 GPA and had graded above average in Military Bearing by both his flight and ground school instructors. Impressive! I found myself cheering for the young man.

There had been several other Marine cadets to finish Primary Flight about the same time as Eddie and they too were awaiting transfers, anticipating orders either to Meridian for jets or Whiting for multi-engine craft or helicopters. Eddie's orders finally arrived and he was instructed to report to the Cadet Barracks, Bldg 442, Whiting Field, Milton, Florida. It meant he was about to enter the multi-engine or helicopter pipeline, neither of which he wanted. He wanted jets! Checking with the other Marine cadets, he found that they too had orders to Whiting Field with the same consequence.

Disillusioned, discouraged, and unsatisfied with his assignment, Eddie made an immediate request to see the Commanding Officer of The Marine Air Training Detachment, NAS Pensacola. Once granted this request, he thought he would bluff his way to Meridian by telling the C.O. he wanted to Drop on Request from the program if not given what he thought he deserved.

Lieutenant Colonel Ronald A. Chadwick, his Commanding Officer, listened to Eddie's prepared speech, hoping it would be at least somewhat original. It wasn't. Most of what he had to say he had heard previously from cadets who had dared to walk through his door. Once Eddie had concluded his presentation, Col. Chadwick issued a command. "Turn around. Do you see Sgt. Fisher working there at his desk"?

Eddie replied in a feeble murmur, "Yes, Sir."

"If you challenge my orders again, Sgt. Fisher will be assisting me in facilitating the paperwork for your immediate transfer to Camp LeJeune for Advanced Infantry Training. Go out to Whiting or introduce yourself to Sgt. Fisher. He'll see to your transfer to FMF (Fleet Marine Force, LeJeune). Now get out of my office."

Without looking at Sgt. Fisher, Eddie gathered his wits, placed his tail between his legs, and decided Whiting didn't sound so bad after all. He would prepare for the inevitable… multi-engine or helicopters verses infantry training at Camp LeJeune. Sgt. Fisher smiled and waved goodbye as Eddie left the administrative area. He'd heard the whole thing.

CHAPTER 16
MILTON/WHITING, SOUTH FIELD

All Eddie knew about Milton, Florida, and Whiting Field was that it was approximately 20 miles northeast of Pensacola. The deserted country road that made its way to Milton from Pensacola, or visa-versa, was unfriendly and forbidding to those that had the need to be one place or the other. The never-ending search for women of the night, the drinking of spirits at Pensacola pubs, and a mishmash of speed and drunkenness could easily bring an end to a promising life if one weren't careful.

Milton itself is a small town not far from the Blackwater River, a waterway that was used in its early years by the local populace to transport timber, provisions, and equipment needed to support the town in manufacturing, farming, and paper goods. With World War II approaching the Navy built N.A.S. Whiting and a number of outlying fields to support the needs of future Naval Aviators. Milton grew to house approximately 1,500 residents.

Checking into Building 442 and after entering his assigned room Eddie noticed a significant difference in his room at VT-2 in respect to his room at VT-1. The room was a lot larger, about 8'x 10' with a walk-in closet. The room itself was furnished with a dresser, a desk with an attached

lamp, a small end table, and a rack. An unexpected feature was a sink in one corner of the room. Attached to the wall above the sink was a mirrored medicine cabinet. The only thing the room lacked was the private shower. Eddie would have to go down the passageway to a communal shower. At least it had individual stalls with shower curtains for a small degree of privacy. The lack of a roommate for the first time since boot camp was certainly welcome, too. It meant not sharing his space with anyone and that he could be at ease with any timetable he wanted to keep without interfering with another person's habits.

After checking in with the OD he was instructed to go to the Academic Building, find out what were to be his courses, and when they were to begin. As he suspected, they were the standard intros to the aircraft, its engine, advanced courses in navigation, and a course in radio instruments. His class had 10 other students. Several had been waiting for five warm bodies coming from Saufley to fill in the required vacancies to begin a new class. All in all, everyone was ready to start a new stage on the road to becoming a Naval Aviator.

Classes were demanding and made each day more tiresome than the last. Grades were immaterial as all of the members were committed to Multi Engine or Helos. Passing grades were still 70; anything over that was a bonus. GPA meant only the order you were from top to bottom. Being at the top meant you were first in line to pick where you would like to be stationed after receiving your commission and wings. Top dogs get first pick. Eddie wanted West Coast.

The T-28 was a major step up from the T-34. Built by North American, the T-28 has a gross weight of 8,600 pounds, has the Wright Cyclone Radial engine R-1820 that developed 1,425 horsepower. It carries 178 gallons of fuel and burns 50 gallons per hour, meaning it can be airborne for about 3.5 hours. It cruises at 180 knots and has a never-exceed speed of 340 knots. It is deemed equivalent to most early WW ll aircraft.

Eddie breezed through the early stages of training in transition, acrobatics, basic instruments, formation, gunnery, and radio instruments. A cross-country to Marine Corps Station El Toro, California, completed his requirements for a white card in Radio Navigation. His basic instrument card meant he was qualified to go on "cross-countries" without an instructor. His next step in training was a transfer to VT-5 and carrier qualifications. He was well on his way to becoming a Naval Aviator.

DIARY ENTRY
Weeding Us Out

Three other students and I just completed the combined stages of Formation, Gunnery, and Instruments. Lost two additional cadets out of class 3-63 during Formation Training. The original number of students in our class was 25. We've lost seven and approximately 30% have gone by the wayside. During indoctrination, in our initial class in Pre-Flight, I remember the instructor saying that the highest rate of failure would be in three segments of our training; Basic Instruments, Formation, and Carrier Qualifications. Only one in 50 fail academically.

The four of us, all MarCads, are to report to Flt 15's Ready Room, Whiting Field, at 0800 tomorrow. We were told to pick up our training manuals at the Training Center NAS Saufley Field. These paperback books detailed the syllabus and required procedures from the first through the 13th flights on Carrier Qualifications, CQ1 - CQ13.

The only information the four of us received about our instructors were that they are all Marine Captains USMC, not Reservists USMCR. They are career officers with up to 10 years of service behind them. In other words… perfectionists. While in the fleet flying in a squadron, two were A4 pilots, the other two flew F4s. "A" means attack, ground support of troops; "F" means fighter interceptors.

My instructor flew A4s. Name is Albert Raymond Rideout, Captain USMC. Drinks Jack Daniels Black label. Has a nick name "Downer."

Wonder why? Just my luck. He's a boozing A4 driver stuck in the training command, infuriated by the lack of talent coming through the program. First thing I'll do tonight is go to the local liquor store and get him a treat: Jack Daniels. Sure hope he's not a screamer. My gunnery instructor passed along to me Captain Rideout's personality traits as I was checking out. He said, "Blizzard, beware."

Having a couple of hours to spare I drove over to NAS Mainside and found myself standing on the dock looking at the USS Antietam. She's the carrier assigned to the Naval Training Command whose primary purpose is to qualify students in their initial carrier landings. At the moment the Antietam is in port receiving fuel and supplies. I promised myself then and there that I would answer her beckoning call and make my first arrested landing on her flight deck somewhere in the Gulf of Mexico within the next couple of weeks.

When I was in Primary flight at Saufley Field out on a solo flight, I saw the Antietam making her way out of Pensacola Bay into the gulf. How tiny she looked as she progressed southeast. I couldn't help but wonder how many cadets were about to make their first landing aboard her deck and how many more had preceded them.

Reading her history later in my room I learned she was an Essex Class Carrier. Beam 93, angled flight deck, 153.9 feet, four arresting cables, length 888.5, has a crew of 3,448, and reaches top speed of 33 knots. Painted on her flight deck are two letters and two numbers: CV 36. We are told to check our numbers. Land on the wrong deck at sea other

than wartime, they'll paint your aircraft pink, fill her up with gas, and send you on your way. Returning to your own ship with a pink aircraft could be embarrassing. I'll be looking for CV 36 while on final approach.

For the past three hours I've been studying in my room at the cadet barracks at Whiting all the procedures for CQ 1-3. I've also been reading about the mirrored lighting system we use on our approaches as we're coming in for a landing aboard ship. It's called the Optical Landing System or OLS. It gives me a visual position on the landing glide slope. Located on the left side of the angled flight deck and while inbound on the approach for landing, I am supposed to see two horizontal rows of green lights. When approximately on the glide path an orange light (the meatball, as it's called) will come into view on the mirror between the two rows of green lights, indicating I am either high or low on the glide slope. If the meatball is aligned with the green lights I am on G/P. If I am high, the meatball will be above the green lights, if I am low, the ball is below the green lights, and if very low the meatball turns red.

We are to have 12 training flights at Barin Field, an auxiliary field located about 21 miles to the west south west of Pensacola. Originally Barin Field was the Foley Municipal Airport and has been leased by the Department of the Navy since 1942 from Foley, Alabama. Temporary buildings were constructed to house the units involved in training torpedo bomber pilots and fighter pilots throughout WW ll.

The field itself has four asphalt runways, giving us the use of eight dif-

ferent approaches depending upon the wind direction. The longest run-way is 4,000 feet long and always has a Landing Signal Officer or LSO on duty at the approach end of the active runway. He's there for safety reasons and will give wave-offs to students if necessary. All LSOs or RDOs are Naval Aviators (instructors) assigned to and on duty at each and every field throughout the training command during day or night operations. LSOs are affectionately called "Paddles." Today Barin Field is primarily used for field carrier landing practice.

Our flights begin out of Whiting Field, make a 10-minute flight to Ba-rin, enter the pattern, execute about 10-field carrier landing practices and approaches using the same mirrored system that's on the carrier. Only this time the mirror is located on the left side of the runway. If on the proper glide path we will catch the imaginary number "3" wire. On completion of our flight we return to Whiting for a debrief.

Each flight will be about 1.5 hours in length. Our training should take roughly two weeks before we "hit the boat" as it's affectionately called. It is the most prestigious achievement throughout the program for any cadet and upon its completion our instructor will pin over our left breast pocket a double gold bar signifying this accomplishment. We in turn will give him another bottle of his favorite booze. From this high point or the apex of our training it's all downhill and a guarantee we will get our Wings of Gold. We will each be designated a NAVAL AVIATOR, and that's all I can think about right now. That's if we don't go stupid and do something ridiculous that would cause our untimely departure.

DIARY ENTRY
Carrier Qualification Complete

Captain Rideout started the brief today by telling us to circle this date on our calendar as it is about to be the most treasured day of our lives. "Hitting the boat was a certainty and this will mark the grandest achievement and zenith in your aviation career," he said. "You will remember everything this flight has to offer, from beginning to end. It is going to be the high point, the pinnacle, the summit, and the apex of your lives. Only Naval Aviators reach an emotional high that is this high. The wildest figment of your imagination will not give you the rush you receive as you come in for your first arrested landing!"

He made it all sound really exciting. We leaned on every word the man spoke.

"You'll look at the Antietam and break out in a sweat," he continued. "Your heart rate will escalate to around 135 beats per minute. In fact, your heart will be beating so fast and pumping so hard you'll feel it pounding against your rib cage. Your blood pressure will be the highest it's ever been in your life. You'll feel flushed, hot... like you have a fever. As you look down at the Antietam as it glides along, cutting a path through the gulf, she'll look so small, so miniature, so incredibly tiny that you'll ask yourself, 'Can I do it? Will I do it?' Believe me, you can and you will. I've never had a student turn chicken shit on me, so don't any one of you be the first."

Wow, this guy can sure deliver a speech. He wasn't finished. "All of you are ready. You've flown the mirror system here at Barin Field to the satisfaction of all your instructors. You have reached another landmark in you flying career, and the time has arrived for us as instructors to step aside and grant you passage toward this goal. Carrier qualification is the wedge between you and your Wings of Gold. By day's end it will be just another achievement in your logbook. Right now, you are ready for this challenge. You've earned it.

"There's just one little difference between flight CQ12 and CQ13. You're solo. Me and the rest of this team's flight instructors will be in two other aircraft, watching from afar. Do what you've been taught, follow your procedures, and maintain radio contact. If Paddles gives you a wave off, go around. Adhere to all the hand signals from the deck crews. Believe me, it's just another day at work. You'll be on the deck and off before you can catch your breath.

"Weather's excellent. Blue skies everywhere. Not a cloud in the sky for miles, and visibility is unlimited. Reports from the Antietam are: seas calm, wind about 8 knots. Wind down the angle deck 23 knots."

Looking at his watch he said, "It's time. Do your normal preflight engine check. T/0 0945. Rendezvous with your Division (Flight of Four) at angels, 5,000 10 miles south of Whiting. Blizzard you take the lead, Shankel number-two spot, Owen number-three, and Kilby you're number four Tail End Charlie. Your call signs will be Muskrat 1, 2, 3, and 4, in that order. Our call signs will be Classic 1 and 2. We'll join up *with you just as you're going feet wet. Tune your navigation system to the ship's Tacan for bearing and range. Copy all the radio frequencies from the ops board; no mistakes. Any questions?"*

None of us said a word.

"Okay, then, lets' go. Cadet Blizzard, let's see if you can find the Antietam!"

DIARY ENTRY
CQ 13

I looked at my fellow aviators. They all wore the same expression. Serious. They were obviously as uneasy, apprehensive and anxious as I was. My gut was twisting, but this is the day I'd waited for! The Flight of Four were ready. Briefing complete, we rose from our seats almost in unison. Rideout said, "One more thing. Good luck. We'll see you as you go feet wet. Blizzard, take the lead."

The four of us pilots headed toward the line shack to draw life vests and parachutes. Naval personnel, also called "Swabbies," work the line shack as packers and riggers and issue the necessary equipment to the student pilots that would be needed for the assortment of flights. We got our gear from them. Their principal duties are to make sure all life vests are equipped with essential survival gear, that our parachutes are packed correctly, signed off by a qualified rigger, dated, and ready for issue.

Today they were joshing us by saying, "Check your life vests. Make sure you have your shark repellant and dye markers. Rescue crews need to see where the sharks are feeding. Oh, by the way, cooks on the Antietam have been throwing garbage off the stern the past couple days. Chumming the waters."

All the riggers knew we were headed for the boat. They were having fun at our expense and looked at us as rankless cadets. We weren't officers and we weren't enlisted personnel, so we took the ribbing as good-natured fun. They knew we were going to be an important part of the Navy team. As we left the area, they shook our hands, gave us a salute of respect, and wished us luck.

The yellow color of the life vest seemed really bright for some reason, like everything was amplified. I hurled the chute over my shoulder. I tried to stay cool, like this was no big deal, but I could feel the sweat building beneath my fore/aft cap as I walked the tarmac, searching for my assigned a/c - T28C Bureau #140558. Finding my bird on spot 36, I met the plane captain, (a maintenance person assigned to the a/c to make sure it's airworthy) and handed him my chute. I began my pre-flight check of the aircraft. The plane captain climbed up on the wing, secured the aft cockpit, since this was a solo flight, and prepared the forward seat for my entry.

My heart rate gradually built, becoming more intense the closer I came to climbing into the a/c. Finishing the pre-flight I jumped up on the wing with the help of the plane captain and stepped into the forward cockpit. The airplane captain's duties at that point were to assist in strapping me into the seat, making a final check of the survival gear, connecting the radio cords to my helmet, and checking the dated signature on the parachute card attached to one of the shoulder straps. With his duties complete he gave me a pat on top of the helmet to let me know everything was a go and jumped off the wing. Circling around to my left he made sure the propeller was clear of all obstacles and gave me the all clear signal to start the engine. Running through the checklist,

I completed the engine start and made a radio check with Muskrats 2, 3, 4, on tactical frequency. They acknowledged an all "ready to go" in order. Switching to ground control I called for taxi instructions and accepted clearance to taxi my Flight of Four to the run up area for runway 18.

With everyone completing the engine run-up, flight controls, and before take-off checklists, one by one they gave me a call on tactical and responded with, "Checklists complete and ready to go." With a lump in my throat I called the tower for a take-off Flight of Four. Receiving a clearance for take-off I taxied onto the runway. Aligning my nose wheel on the centerline of runway 18, I jotted down the time on my kneepad 0946, took a deep breath and added full power to my aircraft's engine. Surging forward, I was airborne with the gear in the wheel well within seconds. God, it was a rush!

By 0950, the four of us, Muskrats 1, 2, 3, and 4, were joining up at angels 5, south of Whiting Field, heading southeast on a heading of 150 degrees to rendezvous with our instructors in Classics 1 and 2. Crossing the beach and going feet wet, both Classics 1 and 2 were exactly where they said they'd be and joined up on us slightly to the left and to the rear about quarter mile away. All was a go.

I tuned in the ship's TACAN, centered the navigation needle on the compass for a direct heading and read the DME to be 10 miles out dead ahead. Using hand signals I instructed the flight to switch to ship's frequency and called the Antietam for entry into the break for flight of four. Using head and hand signals, Muskrats 2, 3, 4 moved into an ech-elon formation. On my command we began a descent to 1,000 feet on a direct heading to pass abeam the ship on heading and altitude.

As we approached the Antietam I wondered what my wingmen were thinking. Were they as anxious and unsure like me? Did they feel the same sensations I felt at the moment? Certainly that ship in the distance had to look to them as she looked to me... a miniature reproduction of a model carrier floating on a sapphire reservoir. Captain Rideout prom-ised us that she'd look tiny until we crossed her wake, picked up the meatball, and gradually got closer to the fantail.

As we approached the ship I set us up to pass slightly abeam of the ship and on the same course. Passing abeam and flying outbound on the ship's heading for approximately 10 seconds, I gave the kiss off to Muskrat 2, 3, 4 and broke left. I slowed the airspeed below the max landing gear extend speed, dropped the gear, and started the landing checklist. At this point I aligned my aircraft a wingtip distance abeam the Antietam on a downwind leg, flying the reversal of the ship's course. With the landing check completed I could feel beads of sweat as they roll down my neck. My heart was really pumping.

Turning back to the ship and crossing the ship's wake on final approach I picked up the ship's mirror and called "Meatball" to the LSO. Lev-eling my wings I was dead on glide/path, airspeed, and centerline to the angle deck. Suddenly, Paddles gave me wave off by firing a flare across my flight path. I added full power, executed the go-around, and set myself up to re-enter the pattern. I had been trained and briefed on wave-off procedures, but certainly was not expecting one on my initial approach. I had been on glide/path, airspeed, in the grove, and was suspicious of why I had been given a go-around. Where had I gone wrong?

I could worry about it later and as I turned back left to the downwind leg I noticed Muskrats 2 had gotten a wave off too. It became obvious that the ship's Air Boss made it mandatory standard operating procedure that all students get a go-around on their first approach to the ship. My next six approaches were all touch and goes, tail hook up. The seventh approach came to a conclusion with my first arrested landing. Gliding in over the fantail, my eyes fixed on the meatball and the LSO. I got the cut. I closed the throttle and as the a/c settled onto the flight deck I caught a wire and came to an abrupt stop. Looking to my right, I spotted a deckhand in a green jacket waving to get my attention. He first gave me the signal to raise my tail hook, then directed me to taxi my a/c off the angle deck to the right. Simultaneously raising my tail hook and adding power, I moved my a/c to the intended take-off spot. The deckhand then signaled me to reset the flaps, which I did while completing the take-off checklist. The Green Jacket proceeded to give me the power up sign. I acknowledged his take-off signal with a salute and advanced the engine to Maximum T/O power setting. Before I could whistle Dixie I was airborne and back in the pattern. Two additional arrested landings and I was finished and qualified. It was over before I could catch my breath. Talk about relief.

Received a radio call from Classic 1 after completing my third landing to rendezvous my Flight of Four six miles south of the Antietam at 3,000 feet. Joined up with Classics 1 and 2 and made a quiet return to Whiting Field. The only chatter on the journey back to base were normal radio calls. I was exhausted, but I was qualified!

DIARY ENTRY
Aftermath, CQ13
CELEBRATION!

Landing back at Saufley was easy compared to what I had just gone through out in the gulf. When I opened the canopy of my aircraft after touching down at home base, I welcomed the rush of fresh air that filled the cockpit. The air flushed the cockpit of the offensive odor coming from my sweat. The stress of CQ had been more than I anticipated. Returning to Saufley soaking wet, exhausted, and completely worn out, what I needed was a quick debrief, a return to my quarters, and an extended shower. Much to my surprise, Captain Rideout's debrief was a short two words, "WELL DONE. Now let's get cleaned up and meet at the Officers Club Mainside, 1800. Any questions?"

Arriving at the club at 1745, Shankel, Owen, Kilby and I stood before the bar as Captain Rideout told all those in attendance what grand aviators we are. We were about to take a traditional drink, the OVER-BOOST. It signified our most recent achievement, the landing on the flight deck of the USS Antietam for our initial carrier qualification.

The four of us stood there like dummies and took the quart-size glass from the most senior officer, Marine Major McKee. Going behind the bar he started at the top shelf, left to right, picking up each bottle one by one and put a thimble full of that particular liquor into each of our glasses. There were three extensive rows of bottles with everything from scotch, rum, vodka, and whiskies. Every kind of alcoholic beverage imaginable was poured into our glasses. Surely they didn't expect us to drink this garbage. They did. So we drank. I'd heard about alcohol poisoning, so I excused myself, made an exit for the head and shoved my finger down my throat. I was dead drunk and violently ill... with a capital "I." The next day would be horrific. That was my last thought before passing out.

***

I woke up in my quarters this morning about 9ish, still sick and promising myself somehow, someway, I'd repay Rideout for doing this to us. Maybe I'll spike his bottle of Gentlemen Jack with something that will give him diarrhea. All I have to do is find a Corpsman who will give me a hypodermic needle so I could insert the ingredient through the cork of the bottle and he'll have the "shits" for months.

Found the Corpsman, got the needle, inserted watered-down ex-lax. Will give him the bottle tomorrow in the squadron area after he pins the Double Bar over my left breast pocket. I look forward to the ceremony, but I also really look forward to handing this Rideout his gift bottle of Jack.

Ceremony: April 16, 1964

Today I was unbelievably proud of myself. As I waited in the squad-ron ready room for my name to be called in recognition of "Hitting the Boat," I Eddie Blizzard, the Indian boy from Camden, Delaware, realized just how far I had come in a short time. I had been an under-achiever for most of my life, except for football, and now was about to be awarded for achievement in academics and accomplishments in flight. A truly satisfying reward for a once bewildered, perplexed, and confused young man.

I have one more transition to make, one more bridge to cross, one more mountain to climb. My objective is to be an officer and pilot in the U.S. Marine Corps whether in jets, multi-engine aircraft, or helicopters. I am on the final path in achieving my goal. Hearing my name called, I stood up, walked up to the podium, received my double bar, and handed Captain Rideout a nice, new bottle of Gentleman Jack.

CHAPTER 17
HELICOPTER TRAINING, SQUADRON 8

Eddie finished his basic training and most of his advanced training with little difficulty. All that stood between Eddie and his commission in the Corps as well as being designated a Naval Aviator was awaiting him 16 miles northeast of NAS Pensacola at NAS Ellyson Field. The fixed-wing portion was complete. All phases from pre-solo, precision flight in the T-34, T-28 transition, acrobatics, basic instruments, radio instruments, formation, gunnery, carrier qualifications, all stood behind him. He felt profound feelings of triumph. The final and concluding stage would end eight weeks from today, October 22, 1964. He would be commissioned a 2nd Lt., USMCR, and be designated a Naval Aviator the following day.

Throughout his journey Eddie had only one stumbling block, his initial failure in mathematics in pre-flight. He had survived because the Marine Instructor who knew him as a student for only two weeks had enough confidence in him to speak on his behalf to Commander Woodson, the Director of Academics at NAS Mainside School of Pre-Flight. Capt. Graves had an unfaltering belief that Eddie would succeed if given the opportunity. Eddie's esprit de corps was there. Eddie knew he could vanquish his enemies with the same supreme effort he had demonstrated those two additional weeks in math. The A.D. didn't have to give him the chance, but he did. That's something Eddie would never forget. The act was generous and life changing.

From early 1963 and for the rest of his Marine Corps career Eddie would be indebted to Captain Martin Graves. Every honor, award, promotion, and success would only be accepted with unfathomable gratitude to this individual.

Proceeding on to Ellyson, Eddie had learned that NAS Ellyson endorsed its name in honor of Theodore G. "Spuds" Ellyson, the Navy's first aviator. The base's inaugural opening began with three hangers, a barracks for the students, a mess hall, an administration building, and an operations building. The combination of ground school and instructional flights had the students finishing the program in roughly eight weeks. Forty hours of ground school training in the HTL-6 and HO4S, about 25 flight hours in the Bell HTL-6, and 35 flight hours in the HO4S. About half of the total flight hours were solo; the remaining hours were instructional. On most days solo flights were followed immediately after a flight with your instructor. The Ops Officer could schedule a student on some days a solo flight, then an instructional flight, followed by another solo flight. Finish the student program as early as possible. That was the goal. It all depended on the weather's cooperation.

The Bell is a two-seated helo that gives the appearance that the pilot is sitting in a fish bowl or miniature bubble. The HO4S is a transport capable of carrying eight troops that are fully outfitted for combat operations. Along with the flight training about 40 hours of ground school classes had to be completed. Eddie now had to demonstrate he could fly a helicopter. He was ready. He spelled his feelings out in a letter home.

September 15, 1964

Dear Mom and Dad,

I'm beginning the final phase of my training at Ellyson Field and will be receiving my commission and wings around the 20th of next month. I must admit that there were times that I thought I'd never make it. Now there's light at the end of the tunnel and it looks like I'll complete the program as I had hoped and as we had planned.

I realize that it's very expensive and time consuming for both of you to make a trip south to Pensacola to attend all the formalities of my graduation, but I'd be most honored if you both would make the trip. At the Commissioning Ceremony Mom could pin one of the bars on one of my shoulders. Dad, you could place one on the other. I want Rose Ann to pin my wings over my left breast pocket and heart, as this will mean we can finally get married. I love and miss her, and I plan to write her a letter after I finish this note to you.

Let me know if you both can make it. Hopefully you will. In the meantime, I'll forward the addresses and phone numbers of some of the nicer hotels here and will let you know the date of the actual ceremony.

By the way, the Commanding Officer of the Marine Detachment asked me to play football on the Goshawks football team. I respectfully declined. For a moment I thought about it. That was it. Asked myself, "What if I got hurt and then became ineligible to continue in the program because of an injury?" I've worked too hard to give it all away for the game of football and the roar of the crowd. Guess your boy has grown up, huh? See you soon.

Love to you both,

Eddie

DIARY ENTRY
October 1965
Helicopter 101

I completed ground school on the HTL-6 and discovered the helicopter is a stand-alone beast. Everything about it is different in regard to conventional fixed-wing aircraft. Control moments in a jet aircraft, by choice, can be violent. In helos the standard positioning of the controls are done in very small movements. The three things that keep the monster in controlled flight are the cyclic, collective, and anti-torque pedals. What makes this disagreeable machine fly is having your prayers answered just before takeoff. This aircraft is an accident waiting to happen.

My instructor, Marine 1st Lt. William Nugent, guaranteed me that I will finish the program within the time allotted and not to worry. Nugent is an enormous man. I wonder how he qualified for entry into any aviation program; there has to be a size restriction. The guy must be 6' 4" about 195 pounds. He walks with a slight slouch. He's a giant with thinning hair that gives people the impression that he is the oldest lieutenant in the Marine Corps. Much to my surprise he's genuinely a personable fellow with a mild and gentle way about him. Married, speaks softly, and has four children, all boys. His personality is free of the confusion and daily activity that must take place in his home. He seems to be overjoyed to be at Ellyson Field instructing students instead of suffering the frustration and aggravation that can come with raising a family. I'm only guessing what it would be like raising four

boys. It's gotta be tough.

After months of training, all my hopes about becoming a pilot have been shattered into a thousand pieces. One hour of dual instruction in the Bell and my gusto for flight was broken. I feel like I'm tangled in a spider's web and my lover with the red dot on her back is preparing to feed me to her young. I'm spun out and tied up inside! The light at the end of the tunnel has vanished and the portal to the finale of my training is closing. I'm told that most students stepping from a helo for the first time see HQ1 as the beginning of the end in their aviation career. Apprehensive about learning to have power over this beastly bitch is like learning to swim. Either keep your head above water or drown.

Nugent told me to go back to the barracks, study my procedures for the next day's flights, and added, "Tomorrow will be a better day; just give yourself the opportunity to improve your skills." I have two flights tomorrow… one in the morning; the other in the afternoon. Two a day and I'll be out of here in no time, SO HE SAYS. One way or another, I'll be gone from here by the end of the month. Either with my Wings or without them.

CHAPTER 18
THE CADET CLUB:
FIGHT NIGHT

What Eddie needed after his initial flight in the Bell was a drink and some encouragement from more advanced students. Later that evening he meandered over to the Cadet Club to relax and see if he could pick up a few hints about flying from those that had been at Ellyson a little longer than a few days.

Arriving at the club he noticed several cadets sitting at a table in the corner blowing smoke. Listening to a lot of garbage coming from one loudmouth at the table, Eddie couldn't take it anymore. Several times during advanced training he had held his breath at the Cadet Club while listening to cadets in the Jet Syllabus brag about what hot shot pilots they were and how they endorsed the concept that helo guys were inferior students. They even went as far as to say they ought to be graduated warrant officers instead of commissioned 2nd lieutenants and given a different set of wings to be worn over their right breast pocket instead of the left.

Tired of their critiquing, criticizing, and passing judgment regarding helicopter pilots, Eddie made a beeline to the foursome and called out, "I'm a helo driver and I'm going to kick all of your asses outside in the

parking lot. Who's first?" Pointing his finger at the loudest and then at the rest of them he added, "Step outside, either one at a time or all at once. Your choice."

Several of his closest friends tried to calm Eddie down, but it just wasn't going to happen. Not wanting to engage his adversaries in the club he stepped outside and waited for the opposition in the dimly lit parking lot. Cadet Ross, one of Eddie's closest friends, returned to the table where the four NavCads were seated and warned them that Cadet Blizzard was an Apache Indian with a violent temper who wanted to know if any of them had metal enough to accept his challenge. He would be waiting for them outside; come one, come all.

Obsessed with rage, Eddie pledged annihilation on any of the four that passed through the aft exit door of the club and onto the lot. Only one NavCad made the error in accepting the challenge. Making eye contact with his antagonist, Eddie's 190 pounds swelled up with anger and fury. As his enemy approached he screamed something in his native language and leaped on him like a hungry lion attacking prey. Catching his adversary completely by surprise, Eddie was on top of his foe, sinking his teeth deep into his shoulder. That bite would require 10 stitches to close. Now the man tried to get away. He had made a huge mistake. This only pushed Eddie further into the attack. He beat the loud mouth almost into unconsciousness. Finally, several onlookers stepped between the two men, bringing the encounter to an end. Eddie screamed, "Who's next?"

As expected, no one responded. Eddie, on the other hand, wasn't willing to give up. His passion to retaliate had been stored away these past months and he was waiting for another careless fool to show his colors.

It wasn't as if Eddie had taken advantage of some fragile individual or like he was looking for a fight. The young man was equal to or maybe a bit larger in weight and physique than Eddie. What that young man didn't know was that he was about to awaken a monster within Eddie. The man would learn that helo pilots aren't what they're perceived to be. Jet jockeys always thought of helo guys as inferior and called them "weak sisters." The fallen man should have known better than to challenge an Apache Indian who also happened to be a Helo pilot. With search and rescue as one of their primary missions, these chopper pilots were trained to prevent a fighter/attack pilot from being captured behind enemy lines. Rescuing their arrogant asses prevented a long walk back to base by the downed airman or an even longer stint in an enemy prison camp in northern Viet Nam.

Tonight Eddie had physically defeated a fellow cadet without mercy. He made his point. He was no weak sister.

CHAPTER 19
GRADUATION – ORDERS TO THE FLEET

Eddie went on to finish his Helo training just as Lt. Nugent had promised. He flew two-a-days and finished on the 21st of October 1964. Lt. Nugent was there waiting at spot 34 to congratulate Cadet Blizzard when he taxied his HO4S in after receiving his final check-ride from Naval Lt. Carlos Gonzales. A Mexican Naval officer and an American Indian flying together in U.S. government property was proof that minority groups in the military were becoming less about race and more about individuals completing missions.

Eddie's mother and father, and Eddie's dear Rose Ann, arrived earlier in the week and were visiting the many points of interest the city of Pensacola had to offer. The Naval Museum at NAS Pensacola was of particular interest to them as it had over 300 fully restored aircraft, artifacts of all kinds, and items donated or collected by the US Navy and Marine Corps. They filled their time sightseeing while waiting for the morning of the 24th, Eddie's graduation. In the meantime, the Marine detachment at NAS Pensacola received the following orders for Cadet Blizzard from Headquarters Marine Corps.

UNITED STATES MARINE CORPS
HEADQUARTERS, FLEET MARINE FORCE, PACIFIC
C/o FPO, SAN FRANCISCO, CALIFORNIA 96601

HEADQUARTERS UNITED STATES MARINE CORPS
WASHINGTON 25. D. C.

From: Commandant of the Marine Corps
To: 2nd Lt. Edward P. Blizzard 085960/7355 USMCR
        (MARCAD) 24OCT64
        Marine Aviation Detachment, Naval Air Basic Training
        Command, Naval Air Station, Pensacola, Florida

Via: Chief of Naval Air Basic Training

Subj: Permanent change of station

Encl: (1) Officer Data Sheet

1.   Upon completion of duty undergoing training as a Marine Aviation Cadet you are directed to report to the Commanding Officer, Marine Air Detachment, Naval Air Basic Training Command, Naval Air Station, Pensacola, Florida for temporary duty in connection with discharge and acceptance of appointment as 2nd Lt. in the Marine Corps Reserve.

2.   The Commanding Officer, Marine Aviation Detachment, Naval Air Basic Training Command, is directed to discharge you from your present status, prepare a qualification record and join you on unit diary by acceptance of commission in the Marine Corps Reserve and assignment to extended active duty.

3.   Upon acceptance of commission in the Marine Corps Reserve you are assigned to active duty for a period in excess of 90 days, and when directed by the Commanding Officer, Marine Aviation Detachment, Naval Air Basic Training Command, you will stand detached from that command; you will proceed and report to the Commanding General, 3rd Marine Aircraft Wing, Aircraft, Fleet Marine Force, Pacific, Marine Corps Air Station, El Toro, California, for duty.

4.   These orders constitute your detail to duty in a flying status involving operational or training flights, as a pilot in a part of the Aeronautical Organiza-

tion of the Marine Corps, and your existing detail to duty in a flying status continues in effect.

5. Besides your proceed and travel time, you are authorized to delay 14 days in reporting; such delay chargeable as leave.

6. You are hereby assigned the MOS indicated opposite your name effective upon the date of your detachment. Your contract entry date is recorded at this Headquarters as indicated opposite your name and your obligated service will extend for a period of 36 months from date of completion of flight training.

7. You are being ordered to active duty from the above address, which is a place other than your home of record.

8. You will report to the Disbursing Officer within three working days after completion of travel to settle travel expenses.

David M. Shoup
Commandant, United States Marine Corps
Headquarters, United States Marine Corps
Washington 25, D. C.

Copy to:
CNAVANTRA; CNATRA; CG 3d MAR; CG Air FMFPac; CO MAD NABTC NAS Pncla; Dir MarCorEducCen MCS Quant CMC Officer concerned

CHAPTER 20
WINGS AND SHOULDERS

There were three additional Marine cadets receiving their commissions and Wings on Thursday. Lt. Colonel David Larson, the OIC of the ceremony and Commanding Officer the Marine Air Detachment, NABTC, NAS Pensacola, would be conveying to the family members the accomplishment their sons had made and sacrifices they were about to make as they begin their careers as officers in the United States Marine Corps. Without prejudice, Edward Paul Blizzard had prepared himself to take the oath that all Marines take before entering the Corps as commissioned officers.

On the Morning of the 24th, Eddie, Rose Ann, and his family gathered at 0900 at the Marine detachment as directed. At that time, Cadet Blizzard was discharged from his Special Enlisted Grade/MOS 9915 Marine Cadet and immediately signed and accepted a contract as a 2nd Lt. in the United States Marine Corps. Official photographs were taken by base personnel and would be forwarded along with a news release to the newspaper of his home of record. This was all standard protocol.

Colonel Larson asked Lieutenant Blizzard if he was willing and able to take the Oath of Allegiance. Eddie nodded and the colonel said, "Repeat

after me… I, Edward Paul Blizzard, do solemnly swear that I will support and defend the Constitution of the United States against all enemies foreign and domestic; that I will bear true faith and alliance to the same, that I take this obligation freely, without any mental reservations or purpose of evasion; and that I will well and faithfully discharge the duties of the office I am about to enter. So help me God."

Immediately after Eddie repeated the oath, his mother and father pinned a gold bar on each of his shoulders, just as he had envisioned weeks earlier. Eddie would later record in his diary that he was a proud man. Col. Larson then read the following document aloud:

UNITED STATES MARINE CORPS
HEADQUARTERS, FLEET MARINE FORCE, PACIFIC
c/o FPO, SAN FRANCISCO, CALIFORNIA 96601

Headquarters
Naval Air Training Command,
U. S. Naval Air Station
Pensacola, Florida

From: Chief of Naval Air Training
To: 2nd Lt. Edward Paul Blizzard, USMCR 085960/7335

Subject: Designation as Naval Aviator, No. T-8109

1. You are hereby designated a Naval Aviator in recognition of your successful completion of the full course in the prescribed syllabus for this training.

CHIEF OF NAVAL AIR TRAINING
REAR ADMIRAL R. T. CROSS,
U. S. Navy
COMMANDING NAVAL AIR STATION
PENSACOLA, FLORIDA

After being designated a Naval Aviator by direction of Rear Admiral Cross, Rose Ann stepped up to Eddie with tears in her eyes. She attached his Gold Aviator Wings to his blouse, directly above the left breast pocket and adjacent to his heart. Eddie took Rose Ann in his arms, kissed her hard and motioned for his father and mother to join them in a family hug. His father said something in their native language, raised both arms up to the heavens, and pointed to his son. Mother, father, and son all smiled. Rose Ann was in their words. Eddie's father handed him a blue stone, something most valued to an Apache.

The entire ceremony lasted only 45 minutes. In exchange for that time Eddie had forfeited 23 months of his life. He had left family, friends, and a devoted fiancée behind to go through training and earn his Wings. He had sacrificed everything of value and importance to take deliverance of his most distinguished achievement, that of becoming a Marine officer and Naval Aviator. According to his diary, it was worth every moment.

Immediately following the proceeding Colonel Larson handed Eddie his orders to his new duty assignment. Before opening the packet Eddie read and signed his first official document.

UNITED STATES MARINE CORPS
HEADQUARTERS, FLEET MARINE FORCE, PACIFIC
c/o FPO, SAN FRANCISCO, CALIFORNIA 96601

COMMANDING OFFICER
MARINE AIR DETACHMENT
NAVAL AIR BASIC TRAINING COMMAND
NAS PENSACOLA, PENSACOLA, FLORIDA

To: 2nd Lt. Edward Paul Blizzard 085960/7335

Subj: Transfer orders; First Endorsement

1.   I, Edward P. Blizzard am ordered to report to the Commanding General, 3d Marine Air Wing, Aircraft, FMF Pacific, Marine Corps Air Station, El Toro, California, not later than 2400 8Nov64.

2.   I am in receipt of these orders 0930 24Oct64.

2nd Lt. Edward P. Blizzard

After signing and accepting his orders Eddie looked at his parents and Rose Ann. They could read his expression. He hadn't received the orders he'd hoped for. He had requested his first assignment to be at the Marine Corps Air Station Beaufort, South Carolina, so he could be close to his home and parents. It was not to be. Eddie would learn to request duty stations in reverse order of preference, as the needs of the service are never close to home.

Rose Ann had completed her sophomore year at Wellington, planning to be married when Eddie finished the program. She had applied to The University of South Carolina in Beaufort. She was accepted. All that remained was planning the day and time of her wedding. Everything had fallen into place, everything except where Eddie was to be stationed and how much leave he would be allowed. They had a total of 14 days, which wasn't enough time to make their plans fit into place. What do they say about the best-laid plans of mice and men?

Rose Ann and Eddie decided it would be best for Eddie to take a short leave and return to Camden. This would let he and Rose Ann reconnect, restructure their plans, and make across-the-board changes without hasty decisions. They decided it might be for the best. They would have the rest of their lives to make their dreams come truc, to be married and to create a life together. They would wait.

Arriving home on the 26th Eddie was surprised by his parents' welcome home party. In attendance were Rose Ann's parents, her brother Vic, close friends, and former classmates, teachers, and coaches. The handsome young Native American Marine gave promise of things to come as he stood before them in his winter green uniform adorned with his Wings of Gold and an expert rifle badge. Partygoers hurled hundreds of questions in Eddie's direction. It was hard to answer them all.

The event was filled with laughter, tears, pats on the back, and concerns of the war on the other side of the world. Where would the conflict in Viet Nam take Eddie? Already the war had touched the Camden area.

Two young men who just months before had been driving tractors, baling hay, picking tomatoes, laughing and carrying on in the fields were now gone forever. This tiny town of Camden, where no one locked their doors or windows at night, was taking on a new burden. All their young men were being touched by war.

While chatting with friends, Rubic stood on his left, looking up at his master. If dogs could talk, this Beagle would tell anyone at the party that his Eddie was back for good, just like the old days. Turning his head from side to side and placing his ear upward toward his master Rubic put forward the opinion he was conscious of everything going on around him. Eddie wondered if he could leave his faithful companion behind again or would the camaraderie of their past be too great to walk away. Rose Ann, marriage, the war, and Rubic all had to be dealt with and soon.

As Eddie mingled with his guests who made toasts and agreed that Eddie was going to be another legend in Apache history, he was almost in disbelief that he was going to be hitting the road again in days. He was filled with questions he couldn't answer. What would be his legacy? He didn't know it then but before his career would come to an end, his people and all who knew him would have been proud to embrace him as a member of their family or someone they had known in their lifetime. His father ended the party by telling Eddie, "The gods know you. They look upon you with pleasure and approval. May the sun warm you. Be frightened of no man."

Rose Ann convinced Eddie to proceed to California and his new duty station without her. Finding a home or apartment where they could live comfortably in their new surroundings and establish a few relationships with which they could socialize would take a few months. Eddie had to settle in at his new duty station and establish a routine. Then he would marry Rose Ann and they would start their new life together.

DIARY ENTRY
Marine Corps Air Station
Santa Ana, California

Purchased myself a 1959 Ford Galaxy. Two-door vehicle. Blue and white. Said my goodbyes to Rose Ann and my folks. Actually shed a tear as I patted Rubic on the head just before I left. All tolled, it was almost a five-day trip to California. Before leaving I asked Rose Ann's mom and dad to make all the arrangements for the wedding. We decided Rubic would be coming along with us after we marry.

The trip was monotonous. Must have driven 400 miles without making a turn in Texas. Straight roads, hour after hour, town after town, city after city. Highway Patrol all along the roads. Put the miles behind me most of the day and well into the night. Stopping to get some sleep at roadside rest areas or to get food and gas along the way was the only time I stopped.

I arrived at MCAS Santa Ana on the fifth day of the trip at approximately 1230 exhausted, washed-out, and depleted of all energy. It took everything I had to check in at Group HQ. After passing the copy of my orders along with my Service Record Book, the Group Administration Officer at S1 (general offices) gave me a check-in directory of all the departments I needed to complete to register my existence on base. I was ordered to return to S1 for assignment the following afternoon and no later than 1300.

The first place I saw on the checklist was the Bachelors Officers Quarters or BOQ. Checked in and received my room assignment, unpacked all my gear, took a short nap, then went to the Officers Club for an early dinner. Returned to the BOQ and slept for the next nine hours.

Up bright and early the next morning, 0700. Had chow, continued my check in – dental, hospital, flight equipment, Officers Mess, disbursing for travel expenses, etc. etc. etc., then back to Marine Air Group 36 HQ for what I thought was to be an assignment to a squadron. I was really excited about joining an active duty unit.

Arriving at the group offices the Administration Officer took me over to a large billboard that listed the various squadrons and told me to look it over and see what unit I wanted to join. All personnel attached to the various squadrons were listed under the squadron's name/number from the highest rank to the lowest. The Commanding Officers of the Squadrons were lieutenant colonels; department heads were majors. The rest of the personnel listed were the most senior captains down to the lowest ranking 2nd lieutenants. I looked for a few that I might have known from the training command.

While perusing the board someone yelled, "Attention on Deck!" In walked Brigadier General Walters, Chief of Staff, Military Assistance Advisory Group (MAAG), Vietnam, along with Colonel William Matson, the Commanding Officer of Marine Air Group 36. MAG 36, MCAS Santa Ana, consisting of five Helicopter Transport Squadrons and their support units were part of the 3rd Marine Air Wing, 3rd Marine Expedi-

tionary Force. Without any knowledge on my part, two squadrons were about to be transferred to Da Nang, Viet Nam via Okinawa, Japan.

This was the first time I had seen any officer over the rank of lieutenant colonel. At that particular moment, I was speechless. I was standing in the same room with a General. Colonel Matson said something to one of the staff officers who immediately retrieved someone's OQJ and handed it to him. Col. Matson turned to me and said, "Lieutenant Blizzard, come with me." The three of us walked into the colonel's office.

CHAPTER 21
MARINE AIR GROUP 36

Eddie was surprised that he had been selected as an aide to Brigadier General Lewis E. Walters. Prior to his arrival at the 3rd Marine Air Wing, MAG 36, General Walters needed a temporary staff member while at MCAS Santa Ana and had reviewed Lt. Blizzard's records. General Walters liked what he saw, had a quick background check made for a secret clearance, and chose Eddie to be the most junior officer on his staff.

For the next 15 days Eddie was General Walter's go-fer. He undeniably accomplished everything required of him. He arranged transportation for all personnel that were to participate or engage in the planning and execution of Operation Whirlwind, the transfer of two squadrons from Santa Ana to Viet Nam. The squadrons were to be determined at a later date.

Eddie arranged temporary quarters for incoming officers or VIPs and established assembly rooms for meetings. He gathered and distributed all the necessary records that applied to the operation. He notified all persons that needed to be present as to the time and place. Last but not least, his responsibilities included creating the luncheon menus for all the officers throughout the many days allotted to the meetings. All things

considered, Lt. Blizzard did an excellent job on his first assignment. He received an outstanding fitness report for collectively using the vast pool of resources available to him to bring to a conclusion the groundwork of Operation Whirlwind.

With his temporary duty status completed and his release back to Group, he went to S1 MAG 36 general offices as ordered and was given an open opportunity to join any squadron of his choice. Studying the personnel attached to the individual squadrons, Eddie made a request to be transferred and permanently assigned to HMM 374, a UH34D squadron. The H34 was designed and built by Sikorsky Aircraft in Stratford, Connecticut, and entered into Marine service sometime in 1961. This was the helo he wanted to fly and the squadron roster on which he wanted his name to be listed.

HMM 374 was commanded by a seasoned veteran, Lt. Colonel John LaVoy. Gleaning all he could from General Walters about his new CO Eddie found him to be a veteran of both WW ll and the Korean War, and an outstanding Marine commander. He also had two sisters who were nuns and a brother who was a priest. Eddie wondered how he made the choice between Marine Corps verses priesthood, since he was a deeply religious man. Along with finding several names of lieutenants that were familiar to him from flight training and only after completing a study of the squadron's history did Eddie request a transfer to this distinguished unit.

The following Monday morning at 0800 Eddie reported to the administrative offices of HMM 374 as directed. The first officer tl encountered was a young 1st Lt. by the name of Ron Brincε Eddie that the Skipper was in his office and requested he peι report to him as soon as he checked into the squadron area. Following Lt. Brincat to the Colonel's office and after a brief introduction, Brincat left the area. Colonel LaVoy welcomed his newest lieutenant to the squadron.

Colonel LaVoy never let on that he had seen and met Eddie during the planning stages of Operation Whirlwind. Eddie wondered why he never mentioned their meeting at the Group Staff Conferences, but Eddie thought it best to distance himself from the subject. The Skipper let him know he was pleased that Eddie chose 374 as his squadron and passed along a copy of an official letter from General Walters to HQMC and an attachment, introducing him to the Colonel as an excellent Marine officer with extraordinary growth potential.

Colonel LaVoy gave him a heads up or a rundown on a few of his squadron's mates and asked in which department Eddie wanted to begin his career at HMM 374. S3, Operations Department, was his first choice, followed by S4, Maintenance. Rising from his desk Colonel LaVoy motioned for Lt. Blizzard to follow. He and Eddie proceeded to the squadron Ready Room for his initial introduction to the squadron and its pilots. Eddie followed without question. In military protocol, he placed himself on the Skipper's left, one step to the rear. The two men never spoke a word.

As Lt. Colonel LaVoy and Lt. Blizzard entered the Operations Area

or Ready Room someone hollered "Attention on deck!" All personnel jumped to their feet as the room went silent. Colonel LaVoy responded. "At ease." All the officers took their seats. Remaining quiet, they placed their attention on the unknown 2nd Lt. or "Nugget" as they're called, trailing behind the Skipper.

Colonel LaVoy made a brief, warm, to-the-point, and informative introduction. The Skipper ended it by telling all hands that Lt. Blizzard had been a General's aide for the past few months over at the Group and had learned to be and is now an accomplished kiss ass. "Gentlemen, I present to you the only Apache Indian about to be rated in the UH34 in the entire Marine Corps and probably the only American Indian in the Corps above the rank of E-2 (Private First Class)."

Scattered laughter could be heard throughout the Ready Room. Eddie blushed. What was happening? He was stunned. The Skipper was unrelenting. "Standing here at my right is 2nd Lt. Edward Blizzard, 085960/7335. He's the most junior lieutenant on the west coast in the United States Marine Corps and now the newest member of our squadron." LaVoy moved out of the way and off to the side about five paces. "Gentleman, I present to you… 2nd Lt. Edward Blizzard."

With that, the entire squadron started hissing, booing, throwing wads of paper, pencils and yelling, "Kiss ass, kiss ass, General's house mouse, General's house mouse!" Eddie didn't think they would ever stop. Maybe he had joined the wrong squadron.

As quickly as the harassment began it ended. The pilots came forward with hands extended for the initial hand shake and greeting, "Welcome aboard, Nugget, welcome aboard." The initiation complete, the hazing was like a lightning strike along with an approval into the squadron. Eddie had been welcomed as a member of HMM 374. Would they tag him with the call sign "Kiss Ass" or "Geronimo"? At the moment, the latter appealed to him more.

For the next week Eddie was extraordinarily busy. Serving as an aide to General Walters and now satisfying the demands of being a new member of HMM 374, he had little time to do anything but work and study. Memorizing the compulsory procedures to be a co-pilot on the H34 required inescapable amounts of time and energy. He wanted to be combat ready within the next couple months. Plus, he was getting to know his fellow pilots and wanted them to know that he was a determined, unwavering, unrelenting individual in the pursuit of his goals and duties.

Bright-eyed and bushy-tailed the following Monday at 0800 roll-call, the Ops Officer, Major Warner, called the pilots together and began the morning briefing on flight assignments for the day. A few were training flights, one that Eddie had been scheduled to fly. Most of the aircraft and pilot assignments on the duty board were obligated to operate in Group Order 20 – 64.

Major Warner started by saying, "At 1300, two divisions of our aircraft, (eight aircraft) will join up with 2nd battalion 5th (2/5) Marines at Camp Horno for day/night ops. We will pick up and deposit 2/5 into a simulated enemy area located deep in the backcountry of Camp Pendleton. Coordinates B41340, overlay map 32.

"A Company of ground pounders from 1/5 will act as enemy combatants in the area designated enemy territory. They will be wearing orange armbands on both left and right arms as identifiers. All aircraft commanders assigned to the operation, please come forward and get your map and overlay at this time from Sgt. Prowler. One per aircraft, please."

Major Warner continued the brief. "Mission of 2/5 will...

1. Establish an OP/Base at Landing zone Hong Kong. 2/5 to conduct patrols to the north and south in Grid Squares BT 4004, BT 4104, east and west BT4204, BT 4304.

2. Locate Simulated Viet Cong positions, routes of movement, activity and supplies. Report to Command all enemy activities hourly.

3. Rules of engagement apply. Capture high-ranking enemy combatant and repatriate all U.S. prisoners if possible within acceptable limits and under cover of darkness. 1/5 has 23 simulated captives located throughout their territory. The captives will be wearing white vests.

4. Enemy Prisoners will be picked up by SAR (Search and Rescue A/C) and returned to staging area S2 for interrogation. Pick up LZ will be designated by 2/5."

During the briefing Eddie had been standing next to Shannon

Finnegan, a 2nd Lt. that he had known while going through flight training at Pensacola. He asked Finn, as he was called, "Have you flown on
any missions like this before?"

"No, it's my cherry, so to speak, and I'm anxious to get it going. Need
to know how a typical order comes down from higher command. I'm
guessing we're going to Nam none too soon and I'm eager for the training."

At that time Finn didn't know it, but HMM 374 was one of the two
squadrons selected to deploy in late January. Eddie knew they were
headed to Da Nang in the central highlands and were to fly out of an airfield that, at that moment, was still under construction. Completion of the
field was projected and anticipated in early February. The Seabees when
not laboring at the airfield found China Beach, just to the east about five
clicks, much to their liking. Women of the night frequented the area in
search of a "Good Time Sailor" and the Seabees were willing to accommodate the Asian ladies for a minuscule fee.

The central highlands and its new airfield were assigned to the Marine
H34 squadrons by command authority. Their equipment was more suitable for operations in mountainous terrain. Viet Nam had been divided
into four parts by MACV Central Command and I Corps was assigned to
the Marine Corps. Eddie had chosen this particular squadron because he
knew where they were going. He respected the Skipper and he had more
knowledge about the officers in the squadron then they realized. He was
privy to their OQJs while participating in the secret meetings these past

several weeks. He knew everything from their IQs, to where they were born, to where they entered the service, to their date of rank and who is senior to whom. Eddie knew General Walters had picked this squadron as his first choice of the five squadrons stationed at MCAS Santa Ana to deploy overseas. In fact, he knew HMM 374 was scheduled to depart the Continental U.S. on the 25th of January and wondered if LaVoy had been informed about the deployment yet. It was the first time Eddie was in the loop about anything and knew more about the officers in charge than they knew about him.

Major Warner continued to go over the groundwork and essential items of the mission. "There will be simulated casualties throughout the exercise. Our SAR aircraft will be YK 6. Lt. Runsvold, that's you. Call sign: Angel. You'll be advised type of simulated injuries via radio using the following codes:

KIA = Mortuary
WIA = Hospital

"SAR, return all simulated casualties to the staging area Camp Horno. Actual or confirmed/injuries will be transmitted in the open on UHF 243 to the SAR A/C using the code word RED SUNSET. Injured personnel will be immediately transported to Pendleton Hospital and not the staging area." He wasn't finished yet.

5. Landing Zone in ops area will be called sign Bus Stop. LZ will be marked with a single red panel or identified with green smoke for day

Ops/evacuations.

6. Night Ops: Box lights mark LZ. Land within the lighted area, please.

7. LZ Control Officer will be inserted with 2/5. Lt. Moore, you'll be wearing utilities today. You've got LZ duty throughout the operation. Pick up radio backpack and zone lighting at supply after briefing.

8. Communications: AN/PRC-10 to be used as primary means of communication. Primary Frequency 52.1, Alternate 41.3. All a/c monitor guard UHF 243.

9. All A/C check in with Skipper via UHF after engine start normal frequency for ground control tower. Any A/C unable to go for any reason, YK 4 will be turned up and standing by as replacement. Rawlings, you have standby along with Keaton as your co-pilot.

10. All A/C return to staging area when insertion complete. Await further orders.

"2/5 Pickup time tonight is… 0330 at LZ Bus Stop or the alternate LZ marked on your overlay. Combined pick up, battle unity, mission complete."

Just then, from the back of the room, someone yelled, "You gotta be shittin' me! 0330?"

Warner didn't blink. "Time came from Group, not me. War goes on at night, too, Big Boy." The whining and grumbling ran through Ready Room. Warner told everyone to knock it off.

"Leading the mission will be Colonel LaVoy, call sign, Big John. Second Division lead will be Captain Platt, call sign Fat Back. Aircraft and pilot assignments listed on the flight board. Any questions? Warm-up 1330 lcl. Take off departure 1400 lcl. Depart Camp Horno 1530 lcl. Good hunting!

"By the way, make sure you call your wives and girlfriends. Tell 'em you're out with the boys tonight and won't be home till late."

Captain Evans countered, "Thanks a lot, Warner. Now I know why they call you the White Rat."

Unable to participate in this mission, Eddie was nevertheless intro-duced on the scheduling board to how a typical mission in combat would be posted and go down. On that same board the Ops Officer had him scheduled to spend most of the day with the squadron's NaTops instruc-tor, Lt. Downing.

Downing was the Compliance Officer of HMM 374 (check airman, as their called in the commercial airline business). He was in charge of safe-guarding and introducing the Standard Operating Procedures to all H34 pilots in the squadron. His principle and only purpose was to see that all pilots operated their aircraft using the same guidelines and procedures as any other pilot in the Marine Corps flying the UH34.

Having finished all the written tests on systems and procedures, which had to be completed before training began in earnest, Eddie was beginning the necessary flights to become combat ready. Over the next several weeks and just prior to the Christmas, Eddie would complete the syllabus and be rated as a co-pilot in the H34. The pilot in command check ride would come prior to his departure overseas.

CHAPTER 22
HMM 374

The morning of the 15th started at 0630 with a phone call to the duty officer at the BOQ for Lt. Blizzard. Lt. Colonel Schaffer was requesting he report to General Walters' office at Group Headquarters by 0745. After a quick shower, shave, and then chow, Eddie entered the building that housed the S1 Offices of the Group by 0730. There, General Walters introduced Lt. Blizzard to Lt. General Raymond Ortiz, Commanding General III Marine Expeditionary Force and Commander, Marine Corps Bases Japan. Additionally in the room were two Lt. Colonels, Lt. Colonel John LaVoy, his Commanding Officer and the CO of 374, Lt. Colonel William Anderson, the Commanding officer of HMM 375, and Colonel William Matson, CO of Group 36.

Since Eddie was familiar with Operation Whirlwind, General Walters had directed him earlier in the week to prepare the briefing boards Colonels LaVoy and Anderson would need to give the geographical orientation of I Corps, Da Nang, the mountainous terrain, and surrounding valleys to the squadron personnel. Also, he would assist in introducing the materials considered necessary to the personnel of HMM 374 and 375.

Primarily this meeting was a checklist for departure and had been put

in place to facilitate 374's and 375's transfer from MCAS Santa Ana to MCAS Da Nang, Vietnam, via Marine Corps Air Station Futenma, Okinawa, Japan. All officers of 374 were ordered to be in their operations center S3 (Pilot Ready Room) at 0930 and to standby. Members of HMM 375 were given the same directive with the time of day at 1300. All squadron officers of HMM 374 and HMM 375 were informed that attendance was mandatory.

At precisely 0930, all officers of 374 were at hand in the Ready Room, milling around while waiting for Colonel LaVoy's arrival. Suddenly someone called out, "Attention on deck." All rose to attention and awaited the Colonel's customary at ease. It never came. Glancing at all the trailing figures following the Skipper the pilots were bewildered to see all the brass. They were even more puzzled at seeing Lt. Blizzard dead center of ranking officers, carrying a covered easel. All waited for the Skipper to give a clue as to why the squadron was about to be addressed like this. Brigadier General Walters spoke for the Skipper. "At ease. Please take you seats." The room was deadly quiet.

Introducing all the officers present along with giving a brief description of the commands they held, General Walters gave the floor to Lt. Gen. Ortiz, CG lll Marine Expeditionary Force and Commander Marine Corps Bases, Japan. His opening statement came rapid fire. "Gentlemen, HMM 374 will deploy no later than 25 January to MCAS Da Nang, Vietnam, via MCAS Futenma, Okinawa, Japan. Generals Walters and myself as Commanding General, Military Assistance Advisory Group (MAAG), Vietnam, are here to brief you on your transfer to the Republic of Vietnam for a period of no less than thirteen months. Your squadron, HMM 374, and 20 of your 24 UH34s will be transferred, based, and flown out of Da Nang, Viet Nam in direct support of the Armies of the Republic of Viet Nam (ARVN). Initially, four of your 24 A/C, along with full crews will be TDY to Chu Lai to be used flying administrative duties for MAAG Viet Nam Command. The four crews will be selected by your Commanding Officer Colonel LaVoy.

"Chu Lai is roughly 56 Miles south of Da Nang. Personnel assigned to Chu Lai will be rotated every six weeks with other members of your squadron. At Da Nang you will be housed in the old French barracks on the west side of the base. Those of you assigned TDY to Chu Lai will be housed in tents until more appropriate quarters are arranged."

"Those of you flying out of Da Nang have the assignment of supporting the Army of The Republic of Viet Nam (RVAN) in combat operations. You will be relieving HMM 264, a H34 outfit that has flown over 8,000 hours, accident free in combat and delivered over 900,000 pounds of supplies into the mountainous area of I Corps. Your primary duties will be re-supplying ARVIN soldiers at various outposts in the field and assisting them in their combat operations, strike missions, and medical evacuations. For your information, HMM 264 has lost several a/c due to enemy fire, but all crews have been rescued. This unit has earned a Presidential Unit Citation, 17 Vietnamese Crosses of Gallantry, 1 Navy Cross, 2 Silver Stars, too many air medals to number, 10 Purple Hearts, but mostly, they're all coming home. No KIAs. At this point I'll turn this meeting over to your commanding officer."

Colonel LaVoy stepped forward and motioned Lt. Blizzard to come center stage with the easel and uncover it contents. Eddie unveiled a map of central Vietnam with Da Nang centered on the page. All hands knew that there were Marines flying out of a makeshift airfield at Da Nang and had been for several months. They just didn't know their level of operations, everyday tasks, and to which specific dangers they were subjected.

The Skipper began by discussing all the training they had been undergoing and why. He used the example of the Group Order 20-64 they recently had participated in with 2/5. He reminded them January 25 will arrive quickly and it was essential that all hands make a smooth transition from stateside to foreign soil.

Their personal affairs had to be up to date. The pilots were told to notify their parents, wives, children, and all their love ones of their pending transfer, and that it should be accomplished without delay. Explaining this transfer to their youngsters would be most difficult as they would be unable to fathom or comprehend the purpose of their absence of 13 months.

Colonel LaVoy added, "Lt. Blizzard has a checklist he will distribute to you at the conclusion of this briefing. It will assist you in the preparation of our transfer. It's an item by item-mandatory checklist with a large number of items to be completed ASAP. For example, medical items. Get all the compulsory inoculations necessary for our Far Eastern Tour, complete all dental work, finalize all minor surgeries. Sign and turn in to S1 upon completion.

"In the text of this directory are items that cannot be left incomplete or unfinished. Primarily, wrap up all loose ends on your life insurance policies. It is essential and imperative you have the correct Primary Beneficiary listed on these policies. Address the policies on your car, home, boat, household items and make plans for storage on assets or items like these, if need be.

"Review your Will. Have one drawn up if you are without one. Examine estates or trust documents with JAG attorneys at Group Legal. Document any changes by having your signature notarized. No surprises for family members. If you are in the process of getting a divorce, complete the process if at all possible. If you are single, I suggest you remain so. At least until your return to stateside. Last but not least, meander over to disbursing and sign the documents so they'll know where you want your pay to go, what percentage, to whom, and the date you want to start the process."

The Colonel went on. "In the history of our great nation, no other group has been called upon more often than the Marine Corps – from WW ll, to Korea, and now Vietnam, the Baton of Battle has been passed to us. No finer group of men has been assembled together than the men of this squadron. I know most of you personally as well as professionally. If I had handpicked my officers, you are the group of men I would have selected. By chance, and just by chance, we are in company of one another. I could not be prouder of the pilots, officers, and men of this squadron.

"We have all joined the Corps because we want to serve our country and be a part of an organization that is unmatched, untouchable, and without comparison. In my judgment, we are without equal and a cut above all others. We are the finest representatives the nation has assembled as a group. Our Commander In Chief has chosen this squadron as the one to put in the field in aiding our allies." After a 20-second pause the Skipper said, "Let's get it done."

CHAPTER 23
DEPLOYMENT

For the next seven days each department in the squadron, S1 through S4, worked feverously packing 374's equipment and paraphernalia that needed to be transferred from MCAS Santa Ana to Da Nang. Everything was packed and loaded on trucks, sent to El Toro, and then loaded onto C130 aircraft for shipment to MCAS Da Nang. The personnel selected as members of the Van Guard would be dispatched, along with their tools of the trade, on January 18.

Duty Sections kept to their tasks working well into the evening hours accomplishing everything Colonel LaVoy had ordered. The all-hands effort allowed everyone from officers to enlisted men ample time to complete their medical, legal, and base checkout checklists. The Colonel authorized and granted to all personnel leave limited to a maximum of 10 days. All leaves had a termination date of no later than 2400 of January 20th. Those not taking leave were to muster in the hanger area at 0800 daily and after morning headcount would be released thereafter of all duties and responsibilities.

Colonel LaVoy selected three members of each department and ordered the chosen ones to deploy on the 18th as the Van Guard and set up team.

Eddie was one of the three from the Operations Department (S3) selected for early departure. Arriving in Viet Nam roughly seven days earlier than the main force the team was to make sure that HMM 374's transition to Da Nang was as trouble-free and uncomplicated as possible. Additionally, those taking leave were required to return prior to the 20th and thereafter meet the morning muster and be prepared for deployment on the 25th. All hands were to report directly to MCAS El Toro Base Operations no later than 0730 on the 25th of January, packed and ready to load onto C130 aircraft for transport to Da Nang.

At General Walters request, Eddie's name was posted on the list as a member of the four crews selected by Colonel LaVoy for administrative assignment to MAAG, Chu Lai. Eddie was to deploy as a member of the Van Guard on the 18th and on the 28th he was ordered to report to General Walters at Chu Lai. Unenthusiastic about this assignment and wanting to be with the men he had trained with at Santa Ana he requested mast with the Colonel. The Skipper spoke with Eddie, denying his request. Eddie now and for the next six weeks belonged to General Walters. Eddie stood solemn in front of the Skipper's desk and watched him deliberately lose eye contact. He didn't have time for Eddie's story. He had work to do. The paperwork scattered across the Skipper's desk said it all, but since Eddie was acting thick, he spoke without looking up. "Lieutenant, you're dismissed."

Pressing duties, the transferring of HMM 374 to Viet Nam on 25 January, and being assigned to the Van Guard departing on the 18th to Viet Nam made Eddie bring to an end any hopes of returning home to plan a wedding. The ten days' leave the Skipper granted just wasn't enough to do all the things that needed to be done. There wasn't sufficient time to make the trip home, get married, go on a honeymoon, and then return to the west coast. If Rose Ann returned with Eddie to the west coast she would be left alone with no friends or contacts, live in an unfamiliar area, and at best her only companion would be Rubic. Rose Ann and Eddie decided it would be better if she remained in Camden, returned to Wellington to complete her studies, and await his return. All the broken promises, all their dreams shattered, everything wrecked by the Corps' call to duty. When would they get to start their life together? It is beginning to seem impossible. Eddie's diary entries grew sparse during this time as if he had given up just a little.

As the days passed the couple adjusted to the road ahead. Eddie continued with his duties to the Corps and Rose Ann fine-tuned her schedule to another semester at Wellington. Christmas presents to each other had been a hour-long tape made on a voice recorder and sent to each other the week prior to the holiday. For now that had to be enough.

DIARY ENTRY
Arrival Chu Lai
January 18, 1965

On the 18th I departed out of LAX at 0800H with General Walters and several others on his staff. We used Continental Airlines and one of their Boeing 707 aircraft. Every seat was filled with Marine and Naval personnel going to the far east. I thought I was going out of El Toro, but I was mistaken. Pleasant surprise!

It was a three-part journey that began at LAX via Anchorage, Alaska, Iwakuni, Japan, and then to Da Nang, Viet Nam. At Iwakuni we transferred to a Marine C130, finishing the remainder of the trip to Da Nang. There we stood down for 24 hours to adjust to the time difference and begin to acclimate to the tropics. The final leg of our journey to Chu Lai was carried out by helicopter and a crew from HMM 264 already stationed at Da Nang. I needed more than 24 hours to recuperate; never been more tired in my life.

For the next six weeks Captain Warren and I flew the General and his staff back and forth between Chu Lai and Hue, from Hue to Quang Tri, to Tam Ky, to Quang Ngai. We'd fly to all these places but were never invited to attend any of the planning sessions. We were just taxi drivers. Wait and kill time eating C rations and reading paperbacks. Tried to study the maps around the DMZ area. Passed time reading books about local tribesmen called "Nungs," an ethnic minority. Many of the U.S.

military advisors at the outlying camps used these colorful figures as personal bodyguards. Interesting stuff.

Want desperately to rejoin my squadron and get out of these shit details and horrible quarters they call barracks. Have seen where the rest of the guys are quartered in Da Nang and they're not too bad. Their rooms are like having an ocean view in a major hotel in Honolulu compared to this shit hole. Mosquitoes are eating me alive. My orders are due any day. Can't wait.

***

Packed my bags!! Just informed I'm transferred to Da Nang tomorrow. Nice way to start the month. April 1st. Thought for a minute there that General Walters was pulling a joke on me. But nope. Halleluiah! I'm outta here tomorrow!!

CHAPTER 24
FIRST RECON

The day started early for Eddie and six crews of HMM 374 with a request received two days earlier from the 1st Reconnaissance Battalion, 3rd Marine division. Second Platoon C Company, First Recon Battalion would require the services of HMM 374 to transport and insert their outfit west of the village of Tra Bong at 150845H. The 2nd Platoon consisted of one officer, 38 Marines, and one Navy Corpsmen.

Fifty-six miles south of Da Nang at the airfield of Chu Lai, 40 members of 2nd Platoon C Company were to be assembled in groups of seven for pickup by HMM 374's six CH34 helicopters. Tonight, seven men per aircraft was the rule. Date and time: 15 April 0845 Hours (150845H).

All loading of troops and heli-lift to be completed by 0845H or sooner. Chambers of all weapons would be clear while embarking and remain so throughout the flight. Approaching LZ Harbor or at the top of descent all hands will be cleared to lock and load their weapons. Pilots were to pass the word along to all crew chiefs to tell all hands on board when they were five minutes from touchdown.

With boots on the ground, 1st Lt. Baker and his platoon were to move out with minimum delay. They were to follow the Tra Bong River westward and occupy a position eight clicks west of Harbor, positioning themselves on the south side of the river. There an ambush would be put in place in proximity of a makeshift bridge the VC had built with the help of local workers. The bridge was to be destroyed after or during the engagement. Intelligence reported that small units of VC used this bridge and trail as they moved into villages east of that site in search of weapons and supplies.

This particular site had a dual purpose. It had excellent cover for an ambush and would allow a speedy exodus to the south if all hell broke loose and the operation turned into what the Marines called a "shit sandwich." The escape route was designed to the south after taking into account and studying Battalion S2 reports, screening aerial photos, viewing sectional maps, and evaluating intelligence reports received from the Tra Bong village chief, Nguyen Le Van.

Tra Bong was a small village just 10 clicks to the east of Porky Pine and two clicks south of the river. Battalion S2 had received a report from Hieu Duc District Headquarters that Chief Le Van could be trusted and that the village chief reported the NVA were headed to Tra Bong and had to use Porky Pine Bridge.

After inserting the troops, the squadron's H34s would return to Chu Lai and standby for an evacuation if things took a turn for the worst for Lt. Baker's platoon. If the code words "BROKEN BOW" were transmitted any time after engagement with the enemy all aircraft were to depart the staging area ASAP for the extraction of all personnel at Dogget, the emergency pick-up site located three clicks to the south of Porky Pine.

Baker and his men were to avoid contact during the daylight hours if at all possible. They were to make hourly reports, on the hour, give details of their progress, and give the code words" PORKY PINE" when arriving at their destination. Contact with the VC or NVA could be expected after sunset, which was at 1844,. Moonrise was at 1955 with a moon phase full. They were to be in position no later than 1844H. Transmitting the code words "PANORAMIC VIEW" meant they were in position and waiting for "LOLLIPOPS," code word for the enemy.

Since this was a three-day operation, an overnight sleepover for all crews was planned in Chu Lau using the bowels of the H34s as a Motel 6. Leftover C rations from the Korean War were the meals of the day. Three-day supplies of C rations were onboard all H34s secured in the aft radio compartment.

Each box of Cs contained about 3,600 calories of energy value. Meats, veggies, stews, spaghetti, dried fruit, crackers, and peanut butter were the general contents. The peanut butter was so bad that most of the men couldn't or wouldn't eat the contents of the can. They eventually found a primary and secondary use for PB as it was called. PB was so thick with oil that when lighted it could be used as fuel to heat their meals. When eaten it was used as a medical aid for dysentery while in the field or bush. The ham and Lima beans in the packets were so bad that the Marines called them, "ham and Mother fuckers." They tried gifting them to the locals, but even they rejected them as a food source.

Eddie was assigned to fly aircraft commander on YK12. Briefing for the mission was scheduled and carried out at 0630 in the squadron Ready Room. S2 briefing was standard with the as-usual small-arms fire anticipated during the landing and departure phase of the operation. Two UH1B hogs (Huey gun ships) from the 54th Aviation Battalion, call signs Dragon 1 and Dragon 2, were assigned as escorts to provide armed assistance into and out of the landing zone.

Take off for all aircraft was scheduled for 0800H. YK14 was scheduled as the backup aircraft if any aircraft went down for maintenance reasons. Redfern and Biddle were the alternate pilots in YK14, with Redfern the aircraft commander. Colonel LaVoy would be in the lead aircraft YK8 with Captain Evans as his co-pilot. If the Colonel's aircraft went down for maintenance reasons Major Brandon in YK22 would assume the lead with YK14 falling in as a replacement. Redfern's position would be Tail End Charlie, Lead Division.

LZ Harbor was briefed as a large, open, grassy area with the river to the north where the terrain gradually rose upward about 200 meters. To the south was thick jungle with heavy undergrowth. An aerial observer made a flyby on the 14th, taking photos, observing nothing out of the ordinary. No trenches, holes or bunkers seen. All trees in the area were standing. None were observed to be freshly cut or fallen. The LZ Harbor was declared clear of enemy combatants for the moment.

At 142130H, G-2 Heiu Duc District Headquarters reported one Viet Cong Platoon NW of the ambush site moving to the southeast. The purpose of this mission was to put in place and eliminate this VC platoon moving toward Porky Pine. What Eddie's squadron and 2nd Platoon Company C of the 1st Reconnaissance Battalion didn't know was the NVA and NLF had planned a trap of their own. Command found out later that the most trusted village chief of Tra Bong, Nguyen Le Van, had been passing along to the National Liberation Front or Viet Cong the operational plans of 1st Recon and HMM 374. The VC were waiting at Porky Pine on the North side of the river and in the underbrush to the south of where Company C was to stage their ambush.

Also, a special forces unit of the NVA, Group 554, was to observe the landing at the LZ, let the Marines make their way to the west, and fall quietly in behind after they passed. They were to encircle Baker and his Marines at Porky Pine. Today was going to be a shit sandwich for the grunts of 1st Recon and some of the pilots of 374.

With their briefing complete Bill Foster (Eddie's co-pilot) and Eddie grabbed their helmets, flak jackets, side arms (Smith and Wesson 38 Specials) and made their way to the line shack. Checking the logbook of YK12 for any discrepancies and noting the logbook was clear of all write ups, Eddie signed the yellow sheet for the day's mission. MSgt. Fowler, the line chief, told him that SSgt. Glavine was the crew chief of YK12 and would meet him at the aircraft out on the tarmac.

Glavine had been the crew chief on this aircraft for about six months

before leaving the States. He personally performed all the maintenance on the engine, transmission, and gearboxes himself, and he supervised all the avionics repairs. He also bench checked all the radios before having them installed in the aircraft. Navigational and radios used for communication could easily save a pilot's life. YK12 was Glavine's baby and he was acquainted with her from top to bottom. He told the pilots that he'd bet his life on his work. (Actually, he was betting theirs, but they trusted him.)

Glavine was a career Marine who was in his 10th year with the Corps and had made a reputation for himself as a dependable and trustworthy Marine. He was a little guy. Stood about 5' 6" tall and weighed about 135 pounds. Born and raised in Jackson, Mississippi, he spoke like a good ol' boy from the deep south. Putting his hand to his forehead, Glavine saluted Foster and Eddie as they approached the aircraft. He then introduced them to the straphanger and gunner, PFC Ross. He told them the maintenance log was clear of all write ups, center and aft fuel tanks were full, oil checked in both engine and hydraulics, and assured them she was an airworthy machine. He had completed his own preflight and everything was A-okay.

PFC Ross and SSgt. Glavine listened closely as they were briefed on the how, what, and where of the mission. After giving the ship a quick walk around, Eddie checked to make sure all the emergency equipment was intact and on-board, had ample ammo, and that their survival gear was intact. He double-checked that the safety seals were in place and unbroken. At that point, the pilots climbed into the cockpit, completed all the pre-start check lists, started the engine, checked that all the temps and pressures were normal, then engaged the rotors, made his radio check with the skipper, and waited to taxi at 0742. All aircraft taxied at 0745 and departed Da Nang precisely on time at 0800H.

While Eddie and five other a/c were en route to Chu Lai, Dragons 1 and 2 in their Huey gun ships had departed Da Nang and were flying a course toward LZ Harbor. Dragon was more than a suitable call sign for the UH1Bs of the 54th Aviation Battalion. On each side of the Dragons aircraft were 2.75 Rocket Launchers that could fire up to 24 rockets with a 7.62mm Gatling gun that was operated by the pilot or co-pilot. The door gunner and straphanger had a M60 mounted on a swizzle that gave them a full range of fire from front to rear. Dragons 1 and 2 had a job… to make a few passes on the LZ, try to draw fire, and pre-strike the area if necessary.

Arriving at Chu Lai the H34s of 374 found Lt. Baker and his men waiting on the tarmac all buttoned up and ready to go. It took little time to load and even less to get airborne. Colonel LaVoy or "Big John" as his men called him, picked up a heading to the west and told everyone to go tactical on the radios.

Fifteen minutes out from Harbor all one could hear was the chatter between the Skipper and Dragons 1 and 2. From what everyone was reading it sounded more like a milk run than a strike. Captain McDonald and Lt. Henning in Dragons 1 and 2 made three passes each at Harbor trying to draw fire. Nothing! According to them it was as quiet as a baby's bedroom at midnight. McDonald told the Colonel that they'd keep an eye on them to touchdown. One on the right, one on the left and would give fire support if needed.

Harbor was cold. Not one shot was fired going into or out of the LZ, and all six aircraft of 374 left the area with no problems. Lt. Baker had his men on the ground. They were unthreatened, uninjured, and unharmed. No KIAs, no WIAs, no MIAs yet as the six choppers disappeared beyond the horizon and the noise of their rotor blades faded into the distance. Lt. Baker remembered something an old gunny told him a few months earlier. "BE CAUTIOUS when it's QUIET." All he could hear was a slight breeze blowing through the trees; no songbirds, no creatures of the night; not even the sound of a cricket. It was deathly quiet!

CHAPTER 25
BOOTS ON THE GROUND

At 150930H boots were on the ground. Lt. Baker passed the word to PFCs Jackson and Haney of the first squad to take point and move out. Baker and the remainder of his men fell in behind Jackson and Haney as they made their way westward just south of the river. Staff Sgt. Grayson with two men from the third squad, one of whom was a radioman, was ordered to secure an area just out of sight on the western perimeter of the LZ. There they were to delay 10 minutes then follow the platoon as rear guard. So far, so good. No contact.

Grayson and his two reluctant volunteers took up a position in thick underbrush that had a full view of the LZ and began the countdown. Their surroundings were so peaceful at the moment that it was easy to get lost in their thoughts. They had little confidence in being a member of this rear guard of three. They were Marines and they had confidence, but they weren't stupid. They could only hold their ground a few desperate minutes.

At approximately five minutes countdown, SSgt. Grayson caught something out of the corner of his eye. Motioning with his hands, he signaled his men to remain quiet. He counted NVA as they came out of

the surrounding area and began to assemble at the far end of the landing zone. No time to lose. The Marines quickly moved down the trail
and made a radio call to Lt. Baker. "Blind man, blind man…" Grayson
called, meaning mission compromised.

After hearing this, Lt. Baker asked, "How many NVA trailing us?

"Don't know, but it's a shit pot full sir… easy 40 plus."

With that Baker told Grayson to bug out and join up ASAP. Baker's
mind ran wild with questions as to why the NVA had not engaged the
Marines during the landing phase of the operation. They had to have seen
or heard the aircraft. His only answer was that the enemy knew the ops
and somewhere along the trail they would ambush his platoon. The enemy trailers would fall in behind them and pinch off any exit to the east.

Baker estimated the VC would delay at the LZ at least 30 minutes
before stepping out in column. SSgt. Grayson, and Pvts. Riddle and
Shane joined up with the platoon at 150955H. Passing the word along
to halt, Baker informed the platoon as to what was going down, what he
was planning, along with the estimated VC size and strength. After the
brief, they cautiously moved along the trail looking for a fitting place for
his platoon to stage an ambush of their own. Moving along the trail and
checking his maps, Baker noticed that about one click up ahead the river
took a sharp turn to the south. Flowing southward for about 80 meters it
abruptly turned westward again. The footpath was right at river's edge
with little brush from the bank to the tree line. Baker's Marines would

have unobstructed views and open ground from the brush to the river. It was a killing field of about 10 meters.

Arriving at that bend in the river Baker quickly had his men set up several claymores along the pathway and spread his four squads about six to eight meters off the trail that ran parallel to the river. All his men were concealed in heavy brush and completely out of view. Time was now 151005H. The initial attack on the VC would be made after the lead men had made their turn on the trail at the southernmost bend in the river. The only escape for the NVA would be an attempt to cross the river and that would be impossible. The river was chest high at this point; too deep and too wide to make it across with the whole world coming down on them. Baker's face twisted in rage. He wanted to kick some enemy ass, then head for Doggett and rendezvous with the HMM 374.

At 151015H, Lt. Baker got on the radio using a relay station and passed the code word "SUDDEN DEATH." He informed HMM 374 and Dragons 1 and 2 at Chu Lai to stand by for emergency evacuation 2nd Platoon C company at Doggett. "PICK UP TIME TO FOLLOW. Yellow smoke will designate LZ. No radio contact with helos; single red panel will be displayed in addition to yellow smoke. Red smoke indicates heavy contact with enemy!" he said in a hushed voice.

CHAPTER 26
CHU LAI

Back at Chu Lai Eddie had just torn open a box of C rations and was warming up some baked beans and hot dogs when the word came down to be ready to start engines and move out at a moment's notice. Gathering all the pilots and crews around him, Colonel LaVoy told his men that Lt. Baker was about to engage the enemy and had made some major changes in their ops. "We are to be prepared to move out for a recovery action at LZ Doggett whenever they make the call," he instructed. He explained that red smoke in the LZ meant a hot pick up with enemy contact assured.

He continued. "If necessary, SAR will be made using two additional slick ships – Dragons without the fire power – from the 54th. We are to get in and get out with the Hot Dragons going in with us for fire support. The additional Dragons will remain at 3,000 feet and used only if any YK aircraft goes down in the LZ or surrounding area. We were to check and make sure we had all our emergency equipment, side arms, and extra ammo on our individual aircraft. DOUBLE CHECK EVERYTHING is the order… from fluids to fuel."

Back at the Tra Bong River, Lt. Baker and his men waited for the NVA

of the 554th to step into the shithouse they had planned for them. Every Marine was set in place. They were ready. Most had been in this arena a number of times with the same sensations running through their bodies and minds: anticipation, apprehension, anxiety, fear. The adrenaline rushed through their veins and accelerated their heartbeats. Their muscles tensed in preparation of battle. Perspiration dripped down their foreheads, in part from the high humidity, but mostly from the uneasiness of playing the waiting game. It was almost unbearable.

The sound of the water running down the river gave the illusion of calm and serenity, but this was anything but serene. Each man knew this was soon to become a space filled with a violent, brutal, and even fatal outcome. The sinister "Angel of Death" was just around the corner. The men were no strangers to death. She had taken a buddy, a fellow Marine, time and time again. They had seen this sort of action, and they were prepared for what was to come. It was a safe bet that someone in the platoon would die on the banks of the Tra Bong River this day… and it was going to happen within the hour. Secretly, every man hoped it would be the other guy.

The brief by Lt. Baker was short. "Make sure everyone ties down or tapes anything that makes noise. Be as quiet as a church mouse. Let the Dinks make their turn to the south along the bank and enter our killing field. Do not fire until I give the word. Then kill every Dinky Dau Mother Fucker in the wrong color uniform. Let him die for his country; you live for yours. See you in Heaven. Semper Fi!"

Thirty minutes later it went down just as planned. The enemy came around the bend and down the trail. Within three minutes Baker and his men opened up on them. The Dinks looked for cover. There was none. They collapsed on the spot. Most didn't have a chance to return fire. Their only hope was a dash for the river, which was a fool's nightmare and an easy death sentence for all who tried. It was execution time; just like shooting fish in a barrel.

When the shooting ceased, Baker ordered a head count and recorded in his log that they'd lost two Marines. He wrote, "PFC Hadley and PFC Carson were KIA on initial contact with the enemy. Three WIAs. Sgt. Murphy with a flesh wound to the left leg; Corporal Bender with a wound to the face; and PFC Young with a wound to his left forearm. One stretcher; two walking wounded." First squad was given the order to body bag Hadley and Carson, and then handed the task of hauling them out.

Before taking leave of the area Baker gave instructions to his men to search all the dead NVA for papers, maps, or anything that might be of value for Battalion Intelligence. As well as detailed documents discovered on the NVA senior officers, many of the dead enemy soldiers carried with them pictures of their families, their children, and letters from their loved ones.

Baker gave the word that all enemy wounded able to walk were to be medically treated, tied up, and left behind with no farther harm. They couldn't take prisoners; no POWs. One Marine screamed out, "Fuck 'em! They were trying to do to us what we just did to them. Piss on their wounds, or better yet, let's just kill the fuckers. They kill our wounded!" Lt. Baker responded with a steady, "Knock it off" and instructed his men to throw all VC weapons into the river along with their ammo, grenades, and any food they were carrying. "Get it done quick so we can get our asses outta here. Sgt. Gardner, get on point with Jackson and move out; staggered column for Doggett."

Lt. Baker called Nail File (HMM 374 code name) via radio through the relay station, "Nail File, this is Sudden Death. Do you read?"

Baker was holding his breath till he heard the welcome response. "Sudden Death, this is Nail File. Go ahead."

"We're headed to Dogget, two Zombies, three Fevers, W-Hour 1300H. Do you copy?"

"Sudden Death we read. Doggett, one three zero zero." Their ETA was 1300H, give or take +/- five minutes.

Colonel LaVoy passed the word to saddle up, move out, and start engines ASAP. "Launch at 1230H," he said. With that everyone scattered for their aircraft. Dragons 1, 2, 3, and 4 had already received the word minutes before and had arrived at Doggett. They were reconnoitering the general area and attempting to make radio contact with Sudden Death. Using the four major points of the compass, the gun ships of Dragons 1 and 2 made several passes coming in from those compass headings in an attempt to draw fire or pick up any enemy activity in and around the LZ. Everything appeared copasetic.

Baker and his men had been moving to the south along a ridge line, making their way by the use of a small dry streambed. Prior to reaching their pick up point they found several small rest areas used by the NVA and two storage huts that were camouflaged with vegetation. The huts were filled with small bags of rice, corn, miscellaneous weapons, and one large container of kerosene. The Marines also found backpacks that contained survival essentials, including pills and powder medication, morphine, bandages and several bags of clothes that the VC always wore to hide out in local villages. The Marines poured kerosene over all confiscated items and documents before destroying small arms and moving on. They were about 10 minutes from the LZ when Dragon 1 made contact with Baker and his men.

Eddie and his co-pilot Foster were at 3,000 feet in their H34 helo chitchatting as they made their way to rendezvous with Baker at Doggett and the unforeseen. They were filling the minutes with inconsequential chatter. It was a way to keep their minds off what they might encounter on their approach and landing at Doggett. After landing it was always the sitting and waiting as troops either entered or deplaned that was the most dangerous. Just sitting there like a bullfrog on a lily pad was the worst feeling in the world. It was every pilot's nightmare, because enemy soldiers could have them in their crosshairs. What a way to die.

Eddie and Foster didn't know each other very well, but they were

getting their chance now. Foster had joined 374 as a replacement for Lt. Ledger when "Ledge" as he was called came down with appendicitis just before their deployment from Santa Ana. Foster was the newest, most junior pilot or Brown Bar in the squadron. He was born and raised in the Midwest and like Eddie had spent most of his life in the fields weighted down by hard work and long hours. Their young lives ran parallel with the common denominators being the occupation of labor, toil, and their desire to fly. They were equal in age and a reproduction of each other in size and personality. That was about it except Foster was a very good poker player. He had taken $200.00 from Eddie two nights earlier in the poker parlor back at the Da Nang O Club.

As they approached the landing area Colonel LaVoy made contact with Dragon 1 and Sudden Death. They were positioned at the extreme northern perimeter of the LZ. Baker passed the word that he would pop colored smoke to identify his position as soon as he heard the sound of the approaching choppers. If they saw two of the same colored smoke bombs in the area, he was to disregard smoke as they would place out a green panel as a substitute. At the moment all was quiet.

All radio transmissions could be heard by everyone. Sudden Death had his own radio pack. Dragons 1, 2, 3, 4, all pilots, crew chiefs, and strap hangers were in the loop as everyone in the air wore headsets. All men paid attention to every word spoken on the tactical frequency and there wasn't any unnecessary radio chatter. Eddie passed the word over the intercom to his crewmen to take the safeties off their weapons and be prepared for anything as they continued toward Doggett. In the event that

Eddie was wounded during the landing phase he briefed Foster to back him up on the controls and take over.

Dragons 1 and 2 responded to Sudden Death. They wanted to make a couple more passes before the choppers went in for the recovery of his troops. The LZ appeared clear of enemy but to be sure Dragon 1 wanted Sudden Death to fire a burst of automatic fire to the south and to let him know if they received any return fire.

The NVA always had a trick up their sleeves. They would listen on U.S. military radio frequencies and duplicate any requests they heard just to cause confusion during a battle. If they heard the Marines were going to pop a yellow smoke, they'd pop a yellow smoke, too. U.S. servicemen had to be very careful in what they requested, so most of the lingo used were in code. Code words confused the enemy.

Dragon 1 requested Baker to position the green panels on his command. He also wanted them to place them on the extreme northern section of the LZ laid out in the form of the letter "X." All appeared secure. With no return fire and no visual contact on the NVA, the all clear was given to begin pick up.

Colonel LaVoy with his six YKs broke off the perch and started in on the approach for landing. As soon as they made their touchdown and Baker's Marines came out from hiding all hell broke loose. Almost immediately Foster, Eddie's co-pilot, was hit in the throat by small arms fire. What happened next happened fast. Foster's foot pressed down on the left rudder pedal, pushing it to the maximum. Simultaneously he pulled back on the cyclic, causing the aircraft to rotate and roll. Before Eddie could overtake the unexpected control movement the aircraft was on its side and beating itself to death. The rotor blades thrashed into the ground, throwing dirt and dust high into the air. The engine went to full throttle, throwing parts in every direction, and the smell of gasoline filled the atmosphere. Within seconds the aircraft was destroyed.

Crawling out of the wreckage Eddie found Sgt. Glavine helping PFC Ross, who was pinned under the passenger seats. Seeing that Glavine was assisting Ross, Eddie pulled his survival knife from the sheath on his leg and returned to the cockpit to see if he could help Foster. Cutting Foster's shoulder harness and seat belt to free him from his seat he saw blood everywhere. Foster wasn't moving.

Eddie barely had time to think. He heard Glavine firing his M60. Glavine was laying down suppressive fire. The repetitive NVA rounds struck the aircraft and made it easier said than done for Eddie to free Foster. Eddie didn't want to leave Foster. Pulling Foster's limp body from the cockpit Eddie made a quick assessment. Foster was dead, Ross lying on the ground unconscious, and the NVA were pressing forward in their attack. Fear filled Eddie's mind as he watched his squadron mates lift off and depart the area. He, Ross, and Glavine were alone and felt gravely vulnerable.

Glavine had pulled both M60s from the aircraft along with all the ammunition they had on board. He handed Eddie one of the weapons. It was the first time Eddie had held an M60 in his hands and certainly the wrong time to learn to fire for effect. This wasn't the rifle range. With two M60s, the men estimated that they could hold off their enemy's advance for a short period of time or at least until the SAR aircraft could pick them up.

Suddenly six recon Marines were there by their sides. Dirty faces never looked so good. Eddie and Ross needed help and they were getting it now as the grunts set up a field of fire. Eddie and Glavine smiled at each other when they saw Dragons 1 and 2. The men watched the aircraft do their job to keep the NVA away from the downed aircraft. Flying into the heart of the NVA, the Dragon's two 7.62 Gatlin guns were tearing the enemy apart. While 1 and 2 were hard at work, 3 and 4 slipped in and the men made their escape. It was during the climb out and departure that Eddie realized he had been wounded. A through and through. He was lucky. The round had entered the thigh of his right leg and exited without him feeling the injury and without the bullet breaking a bone. This was Eddie's first war wound. Per Marine regulations, two more wounds and he could go home.

April 16, 1965

Dear Mom and Dad,

Just a short note to say hello and get a letter off to you before the government tells you the Black Horse has come and
is about to take me away. Nothing could be farther from the
truth. I was wounded and I'm now recovering in the Base Hospital here in Da Nang. The doctor says I'll be able to return to
my squadron in about two weeks. The injury was to the thigh.
I'll have to rehabilitate the muscle and get enough strength
so as to walk and perform my duties. They'll release me to the
squadron for regular duties when they think I'm ready and
able.

I was fortunate enough to be only wounded, as the aircraft I
was flying was a total loss when I crashed while attempting to
rescue or evacuate a number of Marines that were engaged
with the enemy. After crashing, the Marines came to my rescue. April 15, 1965, is a day I'll remember for the rest of my
life. We'll sit by the fire pit on my return and we'll talk about
this day's events. Please DO NOT give out any information to
Rose Ann, as she'd really be upset.

The hospital ward is not very fashionable but it is comfortable though filled to capacity. Most of the wounded are field
Marines mixed in with some aviation air crewmen. There's always at least one luminary individual everywhere you go who

will keep all those around him laughing. There's this fellow from upstate New York with a very thick accent that is reminiscent of someone who comes from Brooklyn. At times he sounds like he's speaking in tongues. He's a megastar when it comes to telling jokes and making people laugh. He's in the wrong profession and someday I'll probably see him performing with the USO. His name is Royal O'Bannion. We all call him THE KING.

I have to rush off as I have a rehab scheduled. Tell all I said hello and not to worry. When I return to the squadron I'll be working in S3 Operations and scheduling Wing Operational Orders all day long.

Love,

Eddie

CHAPTER 27
OPERATION COMET

Several months later, after a complete recovery from his wound and several warm-up flights in the Chu Lai aircraft traffic pattern, Eddie was assigned a flight as A/C Commander to General Walters. He was instructed to be at Command Headquarters at 0645H. The Operations Officer had scheduled him to fly with General Walters and his Chief of Staff, Lt. Colonel Winder, to Pleiku, an airfield located in Gia Lai Province, approximately 125 miles to the southwest of Chu Lai. He had been up and about since about 0600H preparing for this flight.

Knowing little about the outpost of Pleiku Eddie went to Headquarters S2 (intelligence) to review charts, maps, and the terrain of the area, and glean from the Intelligence Officer reports that would be invaluable to him if he had an emergency. He wanted his flight packet to contain the proper area maps, a handheld compass, a PRC-10 radio issued from supply, and information on villages or outposts considered friendly that were located along his intended route of flight. Nothing should be left to chance.

General Walters had planned to be at Pleiku's Operations Center at 1030H for discussions with Vietnamese Special Forces in planning

Operation Comet, a combined operation using Vietnamese Rangers and the helicopters of HMM 374. Staging was to be out of Pleiku. Today's mission to Pleiku was for planning purposes only.

Eddie learned from the S2 Officer that the 62nd Tactical Air Wing of the VNAF moved from Nha Trang Air Base to Pleiku in January 1965 to support Strike Operations along the Ho Chi Minh Trail. He was aware that the trail was a network of pathways, tracks, streams, and roads 1500 miles long, beginning in north Viet Nam, proceeding southward through Laos, and ending at multiple points in South Viet Nam. The 62nd flew missions out of their home base using A1 Sky Raiders aircraft to support Vietnamese ground forces, fly cover for pilot rescue missions, and give assistance in Top Secret Black Ops.

Pleiku had one runway that was about 6,000 feet long and originally made with multiple Marston Mats (pierced steel planking). The Navy's Seabees improved the airfield from steel planking to concrete just before the 62nd Tactical Air Wing arrived. The Vietnamese pilots of the 62nd flew their A1 Sky Hawks a minimum of two sorties per day, searching for targets of opportunity along the Ho Chi Minh Trail. Pleiku was also listed on maps and charts as an emergency landing field for Vietnamese Air Force aircraft or U.S. aircraft in distress.

The Marine Corps had Forward Air Controllers stationed in the tower 24 hours a day seven days a week. Their duties included the relay of miscellaneous communiqués from aircraft or ground units under extreme duress. Their needs for medical supplies, ammo, evacuations, and fire support from fire bases within their area came from operational units as small as a recon squad to as large as a battalion. The controllers also forwarded requests for air support by notifying the proper authorities or command centers the what, where, why, and who needed such a request, and if it were of a critical nature. At times these desperate requests from the field saved many units from being overrun by a larger and/or stronger force.

Two Vietnamese ranger battalions of the II Corps – approximately 1,300 men – were stationed at Pleiku. Their principle objectives were to patrol the general area and to engage and destroy the NVA as they make their way south. Of the two battalions, one always remained at home plate for security reasons. The 62nd TAW of 24 A1 attack aircraft, its supporting personnel, a small helicopter detachment of four Huey helicopters used for search and rescue, a supply depot, and a field hospital completed the military unit's station at Pleiku. The entire area was surrounded by several rows of high barbed wire fencing, tactically placed mines, and observation towers scattered throughout the interior of the base. The inside perimeter was patrolled 24 hours per day by an unknown number of guard dogs and their Vietnamese handlers.

When returning from the bush these same South Vietnamese rangers are quartered in Quonset huts provided by the U.S. Government. Quonset huts are lightweight, prefabricated, insulated structures made of galvanized steel. The hooches, as they are called, are 16' x 36'semi-circular buildings with plywood enclosures at either end. Entrance or escape could be made from front or rear as each had a door. There are two windows on both sides of the building to provide ventilation and light. The rangers called them their home away from home and are happy to have a place for themselves and their personal belongings. In addition, they are issued cots, mosquito netting to avoid the pesky creatures of the night, a footlocker for personal items, and a place to escape the blistering sun.

General Walters knew Eddie would be at S2 and left a message for him to meet him at the aircraft at 0830H. Having gathered all the info and supplies Eddie needed for the flight he made his way to his assigned aircraft YK11. Sgt. Perkins was the Crew Chief and Lance Corporal Cash was the straphanger or gunner. Both men were handpicked by General Walters for this mission.

YK11 was located at the north end of the field where Sgt. Perkins, Cpl. Cash and the Army crews of Dragon 1 and 2 were waiting at their respective aircraft for General Walters. Dragon 1 and 2 are heavily armed gun ships that were to be used as escorts for YK11. With all the crews assembled, Eddie laid out the intended route or flight plan. Dragon 1 was assigned as the search-and-rescue (SAR) aircraft and would be responsible for the rescue if the General's aircraft went down. Dragon 2 would be the back-up SAR if Dragon 1 went down. Code word for the General would be "Bulldog." Eddie's code word was "Apache." YK11 would not be used as a rescue aircraft under any circumstance for any reason.

If an evacuation cannot be made of the crew/passenger of YK11 because of enemy contact, and a hasty departure from the crash site has to be initiated, four villages were listed as primary escape destinations:

1. Quang Ngai
2. Kontum
3. Dakto
4. Pleiku

In that order. The destination depended on the position of the crash site, the unavoidable course of action due to enemy contact, and the direction of escape required at that point in time. Contact with search and rescue would be by the PRC-10 radio, frequency 46.8, back up 42.9. Apache would report every hour on the hour with an updated position report. If an alternate landing zone is located and is found to be adequate and sufficient in dimensions for a recovery, Dragon 1 will make the pick up. Battery Pack on the PCN-10 has 30 hours of availability. It would be turned on, on the hour, for reporting progress and needs.

Completing the pre-flight of the aircraft Eddie then went about checking all the emergency equipment. There were two first aide kits, two canteens of water filled to capacity, one fire extinguisher, one pyrotechnic pistol and cartridges, several boxes of C-rations located in the radio compartment and additional ammo for the M60s. Everything was on board and in place as well as the PRC-10 radio Eddie picked up from supply after his briefing at S2. If at all possible, the following items must be salvaged from the crash site in the event the aircraft went down. All hands had been briefed on who would grab what after an emergency landing if such an event should occur.

At 0815, Eddie began the before start checklist. It took an unusual

amount of time to get engine started, but no one gave it a second thought. It would be later noted on the After Action Report. Engine warm up was completed with all gages normal for temps and pressures. The magneto (produces high voltage for spark plugs on piston engines) check proved satisfactory. Now all hands awaited Bulldog. Everyone knew the Skipper was never late for anything and if he said 0830H, he meant 0830H.

General Walters was the acting co-pilot and was to fly the mission to Pleiku with Eddie doing the navigation and handling of all the radio calls. Eddie was to fly the return leg home. At precisely 0830H the General climbed into the co-pilot's seat with Sgt. Perkins at his side to strap in and connect his headset to the radio jacks. After patting the General on top of his helmet, Perkins returned to his cabin station, hooked up his headset to the intercom and gave a call to Eddie. "Ready to go." With a thumbs up from Sgt. Perkins, Eddie began the procedure to engage the rotors.

With all checklists completed, Eddie began the standard radio check. "Dragons 1 and 2, check in tactical," he said.

Both responded. "Dragon 1 up."

"Dragon 2 up."

Eddie continued, "Dragon 1 and 2 go ground control. Ground, YK11, request taxi for flight of three."

"YK11 air taxi runway 18 or go tower for spot take off."

Wasting little time all three aircraft went to tower frequency with Eddie requesting take-off clearance present position.

Tower responded, "YK11 flight of three, no traffic reported, wind 180/5Kts, cleared for takeoff present position." With takeoff checklist completed, all three aircraft went airborne.

Climbing up to altitude they picked up a southerly following High-way 1 with Quang Ngai being the first checkpoint. Passing over Quang Ngai they continued cruising southerly until reaching the intersection of HWY24. There they made a right turn and made their way to the next checkpoint Kontum, climbing to 6,000 feet.

Three highways made their way to Pleiku, HWY 14 from the north and HWY 19 from the east. Both highways were controlled by the NVA and VC. The third choice, the best or safest approach to Pleiku was follow-ing HWY 24 to Kontum and then south on HWY 14 to Pleiku. Eddie was confident with his dead-reckoning navigation as it had always been easy for him to find his way around I or II corps area using rivers, roads, mountaintops, towns, and or small villages as visual aides.

Following HWY 24 they soon passed the village of Gia Vua and made a positive identification of their position, taking note of the sizeable lake off to their left. Turning more southwesterly they picked up a heading to Dak Luu Hieu, which was about 25 miles further on course. Ten minutes out from Gia Vua the metal detector warning light in Eddie's aircraft lit up. The engine was breaking down internally. Something was wrong. The bright red light was an advisory to land immediately or within a maximum of 30 minutes.

The Wright 1820 was a workhorse of an engine, yet after 600 hard hours of continuous demands under extreme temperatures the nine-cylinder radial engine could break down. On YK11's last yellow sheet the previous pilot had recorded the aircraft had just flown 1.8 hours and recorded in its log the total engine time had reached 575.3 hours. An engine overhaul was due and had been scheduled for maintenance in Da Nang for early the following week.

Eddie radioed Dragons 1 and 2 of the problem. Dragon 1 responded quickly, "I see some black smoke coming from the exhaust stacks. Not much, but some. If you need to find a place to land, we'll follow you in for an immediate pick up and evac."

General Walters told Perkins and Cash to gather up the survival gear, food and water, and be prepared for an emergency landing in the event the engine quit before they could find a satisfactory place to land. Bulldog turned the controls over to Eddie knowing he was more proficient at flying the aircraft and that he should do the autorotation in the event the engine failed. Eddie took the controls and asked the General to reach to his right and above, between the pilot and co-pilot seats, open and remove the pyrotechnic pistol and cartridges from the box and put them in the flight kit. Without any hesitation the General placed the items in his flight bag.

Eddie began his search for a suitable place to land. A controlled landing to touchdown with the engine still developing power was desirable over any autorotation. Being exposed to the dangers of an engine failure and encountering this dilemma couldn't have come at a more undesirable time. Their present position placed them over mountainous territory for the next 20 miles and was densely covered with trees and thick scrub. Eddie didn't want anything to do with an autorotation over mountainous terrain. He knew the consequences were enormous if not carried out properly. You either executed it correctly or you paid a hefty penalty! There are no second chances. Eddie kept searching for an opening large enough to make a controlled landing. There was none.

Moments later, the Wright R 1820 quit. Declaring a Mayday to Dragon 1, Eddie downed the collective to keep the rotor rpm at 2,500, picked up an airspeed of 80 knots, established a descending glide to maintain airspeed and rotor rpm before telling his crew they was going to have to put down in the trees. Looking for what appeared to be a level area he maneuvered YK11 into a position about 100 feet above the tree line. Pulling back on the cyclic to stop the forward motion and lifting the collective, he eased the aircraft down through the trees until the rotor rpm was no longer effective. The remaining 50 feet of the autorotation was an uncontrolled crash. As it fell through the trees, branches punctured the fuel tanks, and parts of YK's rotor and fuselage flew everywhere. As it fell that remaining distance to the ground, it rolled over on its side, and came to a violent and brutal end.

Gathering his wits Eddie removed a branch that had punctured his left forearm and turned toward the General. "You okay?"

"I'm alive, but I think my leg is broken." Eddie aided the General from his seat and assisted him out of the aircraft. Sgt. Perkins and Cpl. Cash were fine; just a few cuts and bruises. Colonel Winder was dead. Pinned under the wreckage it appeared he had been crushed by the weight of the main rotor system. Since he wasn't breathing and they were unable to free him from the debris, they would have no other choice but to leave him. Recovery crews would have to pick up his remains at a later date. Eddie knew every squadron had recovery teams made up of men specifically trained for this type of mission. It was an easy decision to make.

Quickly they went about their business. The smell of fuel meant possible fire any minute. The General's safety was the paramount issue and they had to hurry. Someone had to see the crash or at least observed the two Dragons circling the area. Prior to moving to a safer site, Bulldog needed some medical treatment and so did Eddie's left arm. Eddie took care of his own wound.

Cash cut two branches from a tree and made a quick splint for the General's leg. Opening the first aide kit, he took out a vial of morphine, inserting a needle full of the pain killer into the General's leg at the site of the break. Eddie removed the stars from the General's uniform, buried them in the ground away from the aircraft, and placed one of his Lieutenant's bars on his collar. In the event they were captured they at least would think the General was just a Senior Lieutenant.

Gathering all the emergency equipment, Eddie grabbed the PRC-10 and checked in by giving a radio call to Dragon 1. They planned to back track to the big lake they had observed earlier and would report in on primary frequency number 1 every hour on the hour. They would give a position report and possibly give them the location of a LZ where an evacuation could be made prior to reaching the lake.

Both Dragon 1 and 2 copied and acknowledged Apache's transmission, responding that they were sorry but they had to leave them shortly as they were running low on fuel. Dragon 1 told Eddie it was also advisable to get out of the area. The NVA would become suspicious of two aircraft circling. Dragon 1 told Apache that after a fuel stop at Quang Nhai both aircraft would return ASAP, along with recovery crews, and would be making contact with him at 1100H on PRC-10 Freq 46.8. Unable to see them through the dense jungle, Eddie knew they were gone when the sounds of the rotor blades faded away in the distance. At that point, they were on their own.

Departing the crash site, Perkins was to take the point with Cash falling in behind as rear guard; each carried a M60. Eddie would assist the General in walking. Perkins was given the compass and was to make a track or heading to the northeast and not to get any farther ahead than 15 meters. If he saw or heard anything out of the ordinary he was to return to Bulldog and Apache as quickly and quietly as possible.

After about 20 minutes of walking through heavy brush, Sgt. Perkins picked up a trail moving in a northeasterly direction. Waiting there for Lt. Blizzard to catch up he thought he heard voices and caught the smell of cigarette smoke coming from up ahead on the trail. He backtracked fast to report.

Eddie at that point had to take command as the General was too slow responding to what was going on around him. Eddie had to have additional information of what was going on up ahead and determine if it presented a major glitch in their escape plan.

Eddie briefed Perkins and Cash on what they were to do in his absence. They were to remain hidden here in the bush and not to move until he returned. The password he would use in returning to them would not be a word but a whistle; the whistle one would make when whistling at a pretty girl. They understood. If he didn't return in two hours, they were to report to Dragon 1 their position at 1100H on the PRC-10 and relay to them their plans. They were to watch for any NVA or VC to pass by their position on the trail. If they witnessed them moving down the trail and away from their position, they were to wait 10 minutes after their passage. Then and only then, if all was clear, they were to move out and continue northeasterly on the trail to the lake. If the NVA or VC pass by moving in the opposite direction on the trail and moving northeast and two hours have passed they were to readjust, relocate, and be flexible. "You are on your own," he told them. "Make your way to the nearest and safest rendezvous point discussed in our pre-briefing."

Eddie told Perkins and Cash, "Listen! Protect the General at all costs. Rise above human weakness. Do not surrender to hopelessness. Get him home. Do not let him be captured. He's more important than any of us. If you hear gunfire, remain hidden. Do not seek me out or search out the location of the gunfire. Do you understand?"

They repeated together, "Yes, Sir."

With a glance, Eddie said, "Semper Fi, good luck." He turned away and disappeared into the bush.

Eddie made his way through the bush, silently backtracking to where his Crew Chief said he had heard voices and caught the smell of smoke. Never in a lifetime would he have imagined that he would be forced to make so many decisions with so little information in such a short period of time. His life, the life of his crew, and that of the General's were in his hands. The decisions he would make in the next hour would either poison the well or let him come out of the bush a champion.

After picking up the odor of smoke Eddie stepped off the trail and eased himself into the protection of the tree line and elephant grass off to his left. A pitiful cry came from up ahead, a scream as if someone were being put to death. There was no doubt about it. Someone was the recipient of a lot of unwanted pain.

Making his way toward the fracas he was cautious in each and every stride he made forward. He had to make sure his movements were undetected, silent, and each step he made was firmly and cautiously planted on the ground with a minimum amount of effort and noise.

His heart was throbbing inside his chest cavity; hammering and pounding not from fear but from the unknown and the secrecy of the next turn. It was like being caught in the darkness of night without any light. What was in that blackness that could bring him harm? What was to the left or right? Was there an animal or creature he would scare or flush from the bush that would alert the enemy he was there? Fearing the aftermath of an unknown and the thought of them hearing him coming was the reason his heart rate was running away with him.

Finally, three individuals came into view. Immediately the hair on Eddie's arms and neck started to rise as he saw two POWs who were obviously American pilots and one NVA soldier. Both of his prisoners must have been shot down, captured, and were being transferred to a prison camp somewhere nearby.

What was happening was hard to watch as both pilots had their hands tied behind their backs and were being tortured and tormented by this tiny Dink who weighted maybe 120 pounds. This pathetic little man was a feeble example of a human being. He struck the POWs with a baton and then burned them with the lighted end of his cigarette on their arms, legs, and neck.

Taking a quick look around the area, Eddie saw a small fire where someone had prepared a meal. There were two backpacks on the ground just off the trail and two rifles propped up against a tree. He had to wait. He had to know if that additional rifle and backpack belonged to another NVA soldier. If it did, where was he? He had to be positive this bastard was the only person ordered to move these prisoners to another location. By waiting he would be able to determine and prepare the successful freeing of his fellow countrymen. He wasn't wavering in what he was about to do. Eddie hesitated long enough to plan his attack. He had to be positive that whatever he would do, he would be triumphant and accomplish his attack without incurring injury to himself in the process.

Suddenly another figure that had been hidden by the tree line stepped out into the open. Eddie was accurate with his premonition; that second rifle had another name on its nameplate. He must have left the campsite to relieve himself. When he came into view, he was tying the strings on his trousers. Laughing as he watched his partner punch one of the pilots in the face the man appeared eager to join in on the entertainment. They didn't know it but within moments both he and his cohort would be dead.

The two enemy soldiers were of small stature, about the same size and strength. Both of them soaking wet couldn't weigh any more than 230 pounds and Eddie knew he was just too strong for them either singularly or collectively. He wanted to make his move precisely at the right time.

Being so involved with torturing their prisoner worked in Eddie's favor. They didn't see Eddie approaching from behind. Their weapons lay against the tree, too far away for them to reach and be of any help. Eddie grabbed the first NVA soldier from behind, cut his throat, threw him to the ground and grabbed his startled companion. Forcing the man to the ground, Eddie pinned him easily with his knees, said something in his native tongue, and inserted the knife into his left eye socket and slowly forced the blade up and into his brain. Neither one of the men had a chance to defend themselves or scream out for help. Looking over to the right he saw the first NVA soldier clinching his throat with both hands. Blood gurgled between the man's fingers from his throat before he stopped his struggle to breath.

Eddie then approached the two downed airman. Cutting them free of their bonds, he asked if they could walk, and if they were ready to go home. Reading his name, rank, and organization off of Eddie's flight suit nametag, through swollen, bloody faces replied, "Would you believe it? A Marine."

After explaining what brought him to this particular place at this time, Eddie had them assist him in dragging the bodies of the NVA off the trail and into the brush. The dead men's backpacks held orders, maps, and other necessary information. Overlays that superimpose the maps detailing the position of several units of the NVA, campsite locations, future plans of engagements, sizes of their forces, and when and where they were to assemble, dates and times. Invaluable, priceless information! They must have been couriers delivering important documents to the Divisional Headquarters of the central highlands. In addition, there were letters of a lesser personal note and pictures of love ones. Here were two enemy soldiers, never to return to their homes from the south. Never would it be known to anyone what happened to them, why, and where.

Only Eddie and the two U.S. Air Force pilots would hold the truth.

The three of them made their way back to Sgt. Perkins, Cpl. Cash and the General. Nearing the rendezvous area, Eddie whistled. He didn't need any misunderstanding or uncertainty as to who it was in their area or who was about to make contact with them. Perkins returned the whistle. Backtracking to the big lake and reporting in to Dragons 1 and 2 as often as possible made the remainder of their recovery reasonably uneventful. No further enemy contact.

General Walters and Lt. Blizzard were flow to a Navy shipboard hospital off the coast and were given the best of care in the cleanest of environment. Eddie, for his part in the overall mission, was awarded the Navy Cross for sequestering enormous amounts of enemy documents, acting fearlessly, courageously and heroically while saving two downed American airman captives, and preventing General Walters and his crew from being captured and taken into enemy hands. His courageous and selfless action was in keeping with the highest traditions of the United States Naval Services. He was not awarded the Purple Heart for his injuries due to the fact they came from the mechanical failure of the engine in his aircraft and the result of a crash landing in the field... not enemy related.

Weeks later Eddie returned and resumed his duties at Da Nang. That was sometime in late July. He had fully recovered from his injury. He brought with him a constant companion, the hot, muggy dog days of summer.

DIARY ENTRY
February 13, 1966

Today I had a vision of riding the Black Horse into the hills, so tonight I have isolated myself from the rest of my fellow pilots. I withdrew to a secluded place to pray to the Great Mountain Spirit for guidance. I prayed for my spirit to be safe. I asked the Great Spirit that should I fall in battle my spirit be returned home to my people and not be lost in the mountains of Viet Nam.

The Great Spirit has provided me with everything I need and everything I have. I've requested of him three enduring powers for tomorrow: strength to face the unknown danger, the courage to stand in front of my fears, and that he watch over me in battle. Tomorrow morning I will fly off to my fate with the Blue Stone my father gave me many months ago in Pensacola. I learned from him that the precious stone will give me strength of mind and guidance as I move into unfamiliar territory. It has been my protector these many months and I pray it continues to watch over me.

I have been briefed for a mission that will be the most challenging and stressful assignment I am to fly as of this date. Tomorrow at day's light I will be, along with 11 other squadron aircraft, circling over two specific positions or hilltops in the A Shau Valley. There, on top of Hills 412 and 415 await 80 courageous men. Thirty-six men on Hill 412 and 44 men on Hill 415. They became separated during a tremendous firefight today. Most are wounded, some are dying, and some are already dead.

They are surrounded and about to be overrun. They transmitted in the blind to whomever would hear them the words, "Broken Arrow." Broken Arrow is the code word for a catastrophic situation and to send all help at hand. All attack aircraft in the area have come to their aide but have been unable to sort out targets because of bad weather. NVA mortars and 57MM recoilless rifles have reduced the two hills to rubble. We are to evacuate those who remain at morning's light.

When one flies into the valley he can expect a horrific day. No matter who you are or where you go it's a nightmare. The NVA have a base there called Area 611. It's located just five miles inland from the border of Laos. Anyone venturing into their territory can expect the three A's and one D (anxiety, anguish, agony and death). 611 has been an area controlled by the NVA for as long as I can remember.

Reconnaissance teams in small units, six to eight men and occasionally a platoon of soldiers/Marines venture into Area 611. Their mission is to observe, count, and pass along to Command a count of NVA soldiers using the Ho Chi Minh Trail to channel troops toward Hue and Da Nang. There was at one time a Special Forces Camp at the south end of the valley, but it was overrun long ago and now in the hands of the VC or NVA.

Tonight I had a vision. I saw myself riding the Black Horse in full battle paint. I must write a letter to Rose Ann before it is too late.

CHAPTER 28
ARMAGEDDON

HMM 374 suffered its share of casualties, but today, February 14, 1966, the men of this squadron received more anguish and suffering than they deserved. Lost were five aircraft, six pilots, and four crewmembers for a total of 10 members of the squadron in a period of less than two hours. All were lost trying to save each other and the troops on Hills 412 and 415.

The early morning hours of the day began without light. Visibility during the initial phase of the mission was going to be risky at best. With the sun still hidden below the horizon and heavy weather ahead, the pilots knew they would need the services of Jack Rabbit. These airborne aircraft teemed with electronics operated by highly trained men at the helm who managed sophisticated radar systems that enabled them to give vectors, headings, and assigned altitudes to individual aircraft from their respective flight stations while on location. Jack Rabbits' paramount responsibility today: control aircraft within a specific area and assign targets to inbound attack aircraft on and surrounding the Marines on Hills 412 and 415.

Not relying completely on Rabbit commands or blindly accepting

their instructions, the crews of HMM 374 as a secondary precaution had been briefed to check and cross check all assigned headings and altitudes against maps and charts carried in their flight packets. No flying into mountains during the dark of night or while flying under instrument conditions.

Flight station Jack Rabbit 9 answered the "Broken Arrow" call and was on station directing A4, A6, and F4 aircraft, as well as any other aircraft they could commandeer to targets neighboring the Hills of 412 and 415. Command Center on JR 9 had made contact with a FAC on Hill 415 during the night, receiving verbal requests to target certain quadrants encircling his position. At times the targets were extremely difficult to identify. Intermittent weather obscured the area. Both the supporting a/c and the FAC were doing the best they could to deal with the terrain and local thunderstorms.

Marine pilots turned "ground pounders" these FACs usually held a 2nd Lt. rank that has been transferred from an active aviation squadron and assigned to a Battalion of Marines. This assignment was not by choice but by demand and the needs of the service. The FAC's primary duties are to relay to incoming aircraft the known positions of enemy troops and where to drop their ordinance.

As a team, the FAC on the ground, along with Jack Rabbit 9 in the air, are able to change target assignments almost immediately. Working together, the men on station in the air controls the airspace while the FAC on the ground gives final directions to the attacking a/c. The Controller on the ground understands the lingo that pilots use. I'm sure that today while directing aircraft and transmitting instructions, the Butter Bar holds the radio mic in one hand and the standard-issue 38-Caliber Smith and Wesson in the other.

On the tarmac at Da Nang, 12 UH34s had just completed their engine warm ups and rotor engagements. Switching to tactical frequency and checking in with the lead aircraft YK5, manned by Colonel LaVoy, the aircraft were ready to move. On the kneepad strapped to his leg, the Skipper had a list of all the aircraft by side number and who was in command of that a/c. As they checked in with him, he made little checkmarks next to the aircraft number. With that simple action, they were on tactical and ready to go. Only one a/c was a "no go" due to faulty equipment; that was YK17, the standby aircraft with Keaton and Joffrion as pilots picked up the missing link. As dawn was breaking and visibility improving, the weather was less of an issue as the day marched forward.

Colonel LaVoy called the tower for takeoff for his flight of 12 H34s and asked for a departure to the southwest. With all his aircraft airborne and outside the airport boundary, LaVoy made contact with Air Force Tactical (code name Puma) on board Jack Rabbit 9. Puma issued instructions. The Skipper turned to the assigned heading of 250 magnetic on his compass as directed and set in motion the beginning of a long and difficult day. All 12 aircraft were to fly into "Harm's Way" deep into the A Shau Valley.

Tensions were high. From pilots to crew chiefs, everyone knew medivacs and now a Broken Arrow call were not supply or milk runs. Eddie's co-pilot for that day was a two-year college man who had attended Villanova University and who started his aviation career as a MarCad. Born Italian, raised on the south side of Philly, Alberto Santoro stood 5' 10" and weighed about 160 pounds. One thing that set him apart from others in the squadron was his thick Philly accent full of too many "yeahs" and a multitude of "you knows" in normal conversation.

Some pushed him off as a rude guy, but ol' Santoro always won them over with stories. Like when he was in high school and he would go to American Bandstand in downtown Philly after school to score time with the chicks. Just about drove Eddie crazy trying to figure out what was truth or what was fiction. Guys in the squadron gave him the call sign "Story Teller." The common denominators between Alberto and Eddie? Flying and baseball. They followed the Philadelphia Phillies to an extreme.

Eddie's crew chief was SSgt. Perkins, the same SSgt. he had been with when he crashed in the mountains east of Pleiku. Since then, Lt. Blizzard and SSgt. Perkins had been flying most of their sorties and missions together, bonding with mutual respect. Perkins wanted Lt. Blizzard flying his aircraft and Eddie wanted Perkins to crew for him. They knew they could depend on each other no matter what. The Operations Duty Officer did his best to assign Lt. Blizzard to Perkins' aircraft; that's if they had a sortie or mission to fly that day and Perkins' a/c was needed in the day's operations.

After their joint escape and evasion adventure Perkins discovered Cpl. Webb, a clerk who worked in S1 had been rifling through the all the officers' SRBs. It didn't surprise Perkins and the rest of the men in the least when they discovered that Lt. Blizzard was a Mustang (former enlisted man). He always felt that the Lieutenant had treated his men differently than other officers in the squadron. Those under his command had a little more rope than the average Marine, not that he was lax in leadership. He was just considerably more compassionate than the average officer in the squadron in regard to putting men on report.

Finding out that Lt. Blizzard had been a prior enlisted man and having gone through Parris Island, Perkins respected Eddie that much more. It got around quick in the NCO Club that Eddie was a Mustang; many of the crew chiefs in the squadron wanted him to HAC their aircraft. But Perkins was everything Eddie wanted in a Crew Chief: dependable, straight away, up front… a real tell-the-truth SSgt. No bullshit, no color, ramrod straight and an excellent mechanic. If the a/c was down for maintenance, it wouldn't fly till it was 100 percent operational. From the clamshell doors in front to the tail rotor in the rear and everything in between, it had to be flawless before any aviator would be allowed to crawl into the cockpit. This made YK22 Eddie's preference for an aircraft and Perkins his Marine of choice as a crew chief.

Pfc. Stanton, the fourth member of the crew would be manning a M60 machine gun at one of the windows. Born and raised in Ocean City, Maryland, he told everyone that he liked to go to the beach, fish, party, and chase girls… in that order. When not in the barracks you could bet your last dollar he was over at China Beach in pursuit of the locals. The squadron Flight Surgeon warned Stanton about venereal diseases. "Get VD and you can't go home till it's cleared up!"

In Viet Nam there were so many varieties of VD that the medical research labs at the Da Nang Hospital placed groups of them in specific categories labeled from curable to deadly. Most were unidentifiable and undergoing medical testing in hopes of finding a cure. Two men had been isolated from the rest of the squadron as a result and were in the process of being transferred to a hospital in Saigon that was better equipped to handle such cases. VD was no joke.

Pfc. Stanton had joined the Corps about a year earlier. Went through boot camp at Parris Island then ordered to a Clerk Typist School. Upon completion, he was nicknamed "Remington Raider" and transferred to HMM 374. While on duty he worked in S3 Operations, verifying and making entries into the pilots' and crewmembers' military logbooks. All missions into areas where enemy contact can be reasonably expected were entered in the log in red ink. After 20 such missions or sorties the crewmember or pilot was recommended for the Air Medal.

On occasion, Stanton would be called on to fly missions like everyone else in the unit. At times he was assigned to flight status only because the particular day's requirements for flight crews exceeded the number of flight crews on hand. This little guy, this "Feather Merchant," just 19 years of age, baby faced, looking like he should be in junior high school was a top choice. Guys in the squadron poked fun at him. "You still got your baby teeth?" they mocked.

Four men on aircraft YK22 heading into battle determined in their purpose, willing to sacrifice, surrender or forfeit everything that was theirs for those that needed their help. Marines on hills 412 and 415 had been killed or wounded; some were about to die, and some desperately wanted to survive. HMM 374's motto? "We're Coming. Hang in There!" The men behind that motto were on their way.

As they cruised toward their rendezvous with destiny many things ran through Eddie's mind. He thought about that fight he had with that loudmouth jet jockey at the Cadet Club in Pensacola. That braggart who thought chopper pilots were inferior ought to see what they were being asked to do on this day! Wouldn't it be ironic if that same egomaniac happened to be the FAC on Hill 412 or 415?

Brave young Marines of contrasting character were on those bombarded hilltops, Marines he didn't know by name. These Marines could have come from anywhere… the city, the countryside, the suburbs. It didn't matter. They needed his help, and 12 H34s were on their way to get their asses out of Harm's Way. Eddie didn't put thought to being injured. He thought about the approach, landing, picking up his eight troopers and getting out of there safely. He knew when the troops heard the choppers approaching they'd think, "We're gonna make it. God's Angels from Heaven are here!"

As they arrived at their point of entry the 12 helos were told to switch to a tactical frequency that the fighters and Dragon gunships were using. Right then, the FAC was chitchatting with two A4s, call sign Viper 1 and 2, saying, "Dropped your jelly at the foot of Hill 412 on the western side. You've gotta cut off the Reserves the NVA are sending. We can't let them join up with those already within 50 yards of capping the hill."

This was followed by, "No delay, DoZo. Our field of fire has stopped them temporarily and holding them at their present position. They are not gaining or approaching any closer to our position."

While this was going down on Hill 412, Dragon 2 had been making passes on the eastern and western slopes of Hill 415. Dividing his command into two separate groups, Colonel LaVoy took six H34s to Hill 412 along with Dragon 1. Major Sanchez took six to Hill 415 and joined up with Dragon 2. The Colonel's group was assigned 3,000 feet, left-hand pattern from Puma. Major Sanchez was assigned 4,000 feet right-hand pattern from Puma. The two hills were about 1 ½ clicks apart.

After the A4s dropped their Napalm on the western slope and temporarily stopped the advance of the attack, Puma called the lead chopper, plus one, to immediately begin the evac. As directed and descending from 3,000 feet, Colonel LaVoy and his wingman broke off the perch, and started their approach to the LZ. They instantly received 50-caliber fire from their left. Dragon 1, paralleling the Colonel's glide path fired his rockets and machine guns in an attempt to stop the enemy advance up the hill's western slope and suppress the firepower centered on LaVoy's two descending H34s.

The NVA were in the open. Their screams and trumpets could almost be heard as they crawled their way up the muddy hill. The FAC screeched out over the radio, "Good drop, Viper 1. Stopped their advance but nearly burned the hair off my arms. Keep it coming. Do not, I repeat, do not drop any closer. Too hot; takes our breath away!"

Just as LaVoy was about to touch down his wingman in YK15 with Captain Enslet and 1st Lt. Rand aboard crashed and rolled down the eastern face of the hill.

LaVoy under continuous heavy fire picked up as many Marines as his a/c could hold and made an easterly departure out of the LZ. With all his attention directed toward flying his aircraft and only after successfully departing the area did he notice his co-pilot Lt. Daley had been wounded and was unresponsive. At this point, since he had lost his wingman, he ordered Lt. Blizzard in YK22 to join up on him as an escort to Home Plate, the staging area. Eddie was on it.

One of the rescued Marines in the cabin passed the word to the crew chief that there were 37 men still on the ground, most of them wounded. LaVoy ordered the next two H34s off the perch and in for a pick up. "Thirty-seven Marines waiting for you. Get um outta there. Chop Chop, Hayaku! They're about to be overrun. Most of the fire coming from the west. Suggest departure to the east after pick up."

Colonel LaVoy, with Lt. Blizzard on his wing, transferred command of this can of worms to Major Sanchez. While climbing to 5,000 feet he told Lt. Blizzard to go to Button 2 on the UHF radio.

LaVoy told Eddie that Daley was hit and unresponsive. While he worked on Daley, LaVoy requested Eddie to call ahead for immediate medical assistance after touch down for three Marines in the cabin and the co-pilot. He also told Eddie his instrument panel was nothing but shattered glass and unreliable gages. "Take a look-see visual check of my a/c for any damage you think might be of importance," he directed.

Flying from side to side, from bottom to top, Eddie reported he had some good news and some bad news. First, he told the Skipper he was going to make it home; second, the aft fuel tank was draining fuel at an alarmingly fast rate. He suggested he transfer the remaining fuel from aft tank to the forward tank and using that fuel as the primary source to run the engine until the tank was almost dry. Then switch to primary tanks. Other than that, no visual damage except the aft pylon, which was riddled with bullet holes.

While all this was going down, an F4 made a pass as the next two H34s approached touch down. The heavy fire continued. YK12 leading the section into the LZ was hit by a RPG in the aft pylon area, causing immediate tail rotor failure. Keaton and Joffrion whirled around 360 degrees at least twice before crashing onto the northern section of the LZ. Dirt, dust, debris and fragments of wreckage flew everywhere for what seemed like an eternity. As quickly as it began, the turmoil ended. Both pilots were killed on impact while the window gunner escaped with minor injuries. Couldn't tell what happened to the crew chief. Found out later that Sgt. Pane was KIA during the approach. FUBAR! The gunner on Keaton's a/c scrambled from the rubble and took up a position in one of the foxholes formally occupied by a Grunt that had just been evacuated. Mason was now an Infantry Marine with a side arm fighting for his life instead of a crewmember on YK12, up and out of the range of small arms fire, out of danger, and enjoying the ride home.

LaVoy and Eddie touched down back in the staging area and immediately doctors, corpsmen, and medical staff crawled over their aircraft. Eddie shut down his equipment, then had the craft refueled and checked for battle damage. Everything was A-Okay. In the meantime, the Skipper slid out of his a/c. He told Eddie he would refuel and fire up YK17. He told the crew chief to cannibalize YK5's radios and place them into YK17's radio rack ASAP. He wanted to get back to the valley and his squadron. "Get it done. Quick like a bunny!"

Back at the hills the rescue went as planned with Major Sanchez commanding. By the time LaVoy and Eddie returned they had about 12 Marines still trapped and struggling on Hill 415. LaVoy went in for the second time, picked up six, and Eddie was right behind to pick up the leftovers. With the defensive perimeter falling back farther and farther, and as the enemy got closer, the more dangerous the last pick up became. So many rounds were hitting Eddie's aircraft it seemed unbelievable that everything was running normally and no one had been hit by enemy fire.

Lifting off to the east Perkins screamed over the intercom, "I'm hit! Two Marines still on the hill!"

Eddie was stunned that he had not seen them and immediately started to circle back around for a pick up. With both Dragon helos by his side, Eddie re-entered what most would call the above and beyond arena in the call of duty. Setting down once again and with the gunner blazing away with his M60 they picked up the forgotten men and climbed their way to a safe altitude.

Eddie turned his head to look at Santoro and said. "You have the aircraft." He slowly laid his head back on the crown of the pilot's seat, took one last deep breath and died. Eddie was going home.

DEBRIEF
February 16, 1966

With the mission completed and the return of all aircraft to Da Nang, Colonel LaVoy ordered the squadron to stand down on the 15th and 16th. One exception… all hands were to muster in the hanger area on the 16th at 1800H.

General Walters, along with Colonel LaVoy wanted to address the members of the squadron on the events of the 14th. Both the General and the Colonel knew the men needed 48 hours on their own to digest the significance of what had just happened, to collect their thoughts, and to regain their composure. For their own sanity, the men needed a recess, a temporary pause from duty, and a timely intermission to wake from the nightmare they just experienced. The Skipper wanted a temporary suspension from duty for all the men with sufficient time to regain their focus and prepare for future missions.

The next day, at precisely 1800 hours, Colonel LaVoy addressed his men. Brow furrowed, he began. "It is a sad day for our squadron. We lost five aircraft or 20 percent of our fleet. Another seven or 30 percent of our aircraft received debilitating battle damage, and effectively we are at a level of 50 percent combat readiness or less. That is not what concerns me; aircraft can be repaired or made ready to fly once again. Our most disparaging and devastating damage comes from the death of the following men." He read the names slowly. "Captains Enslet, Joffrion, and Keaton. Lieutenants Blizzard, Daley, and Rand. Pfc. Fielder, Sergeant

Pane, Sergeant Alston, and Staff Sergeant Perkins. We also have had six additional crewmembers that were wounded and are in the Base Hospital here at Da Nang."

LaVoy paused and took a breath before beginning again. "As catastrophic as the day was, and as regrettably painful to have lost our friends and brothers, we must carry on. It is our duty to remember what they stood for and not dwell on their untimely departure. They exchanged their lives for the stranded Marines on Hills 412 and 415. No greater example of devotion to duty or the demonstration of courage was displayed by those who sacrificed their lives on the 14th so that others may live. We as a group will never forget and have forever implanted in our consciousness the date of February 14th and the numbers 412 and 415. It has now been engraved or inscribed in the manuscript and history of our squadron. It can and will never be forgotten. May the story be told and glorified to those who follow us into battle. To the end they have lived our motto, Semper Fi, Always Faithful. May they rest in peace. Now, General Walters has a few words for you."

General Walters was equally somber, "I have a handwritten letter from one of the Marines you pulled off Hill 415. You need to know what he wrote. Maybe this will help you in the grief you share for your fellow Marines that were lost on the 14th."

The General began to read, "To our Angels from Heaven; I now know and have experienced the phrase 'No Marine left behind.' The depth of its meaning will be with my men and me for the rest of our lives. All of us faced the reality that we were about to die on that hill. You came for us; you were there for us. You took us from anguish and carried us to safety knowing death was at your doorstep. You would not leave us behind.

"To those of you who were so brave on this day to have come to our rescue, I tell you all, from the innermost fiber of my soul, the words 'no one left behind' means everything to me and my men. We thank you for saving our lives but are grieved beyond belief for the exchange of our lives for the loss of the men in your squadron. God bless you all. This is signed by 1st Lt. Robert H. Riddle, USMCR."

General Walters went on with a steady, purposeful voice. "Many of you have been concerned about the recovery of the members of 374 lost in battle two days ago. A special unit of Recon, Delta Team 4 out of Chu Lai, was ordered into the area on the 15th and the recovery of all hands lost was completed by 1500Hs yesterday. With that mission complete, I have since drawn up orders for the following persons to act as Escorts in returning the remains of HMM 374s deceased. Lt. William Redding and Lt. McDonald, you will escort the remains of all officers to state-side; Master Sgt. Costello, you will assist in the transfer of the deceased enlisted personnel.

"As directed, you will meet the families or the representative of the deceased in the most dignified military manner at Dover Air Force, Dover, Delaware. You will transfer possession of the remains to family members or a party selected by them. If that is not possible, you will arrange transportation of the remains, using Marine Escort Personnel stationed at Dover to a funeral parlor at the deceases home of record or to the destination of their choice. You will receive additional information after your arrival at Dover.

"All personal items, including clothing of the deceased, have been removed from their quarters, cleaned and neatly packed in their individual footlockers. Items that would offend family members have been sorted, removed and destroyed. You will return these personal items to the families after your arrival stateside. All escorts, along with the remains will depart Da Nang on February 18th at 0800 using a U.S. Air Force KC130. A Memorial service will be held by the Base Chaplin at 2130H this evening. Be there, Hanger 35, on time.

"Lt. Redding, I'll see you at 0800H on February 23, 1966, at the Office of Graves Registration, Arlington National Cemetery. Lt. Blizzard and others have noted and written in their Wills that their final resting place be Arlington National Cemetery, Arlington, Virginia. With no further discussion or questions…" Here the General broke into silence and dropped his head. Taking a breath, he pushed his shoulders back as he refocused on the group. "You are dismissed."

February, 13, 1966

My Darling Rose Ann,

If you are reading this I know you have met Lt. William Redding, as he has agreed to personally hand deliver this letter to you. As I write this letter now, I face tomorrow in my mind this night. Operations Backwash is an extremely hazardous mission that begins early tomorrow morning. There might not be another opportunity to tell you just what you have meant to me over our lifetime.

I remember what a cutie-pie you were. The first time I caught a glimpse of you, you were standing in front of the gymnasium with your girlfriends, giggling as you waited for the school bus to take you home. I couldn't help but think what a special lady you would be. From that day until now, I knew I wanted you to share and be a part of my life. That first day I laid eyes on you was when we were attending grammar school. It underscored the many events that highlighted our high school and college years. My heart is warmed as I think of those early days in our life. I treasured your love.

I'm sitting here at my desk as I look at your picture. You are the most beautiful woman in my world. Do you remember our first kiss there at the Mill Pond? You had been sitting there on lake's edge with Rubic, our constant companion. Both of you watched me fish for bass as the sun retreated beyond the trees on the other side of the lake. After placing my pole down on the bank I sat down beside you. We just chatted and watched the line for a bite. (I thank Rubic for what happened next.) The darned dog jumped up on your shoulder and knocked you into me. With that bump our heads turned toward each other, our eyes met, and our lips just came together. I remember it as if it were yesterday.

Our first real date was in 1959. I'd been working all summer on Mr. Greenwell's farm. Snooky Belmont had been flirting with you while I was away. A couple guys on the football team told me Snooky was going to ask you to the dance, so I better get with it if I wanted to take you. Finally I mustered up enough courage to ask and you said yes. I almost did a back flip right then and there! At the dance I remember holding you in my arms when they played our song, "Puppy Love." Expressing the way I felt and what you meant to me that night can only be spoken using three little words... I love you.

I recall the many hours in the library during study period. You studied and I fooled around. You enjoyed getting As and Bs. I was satisfied with Cs and Ds. My only A was in Physical Education. Reminiscing about CR, Wellington, and you, has given to me a picture-perfect life. The Crown Jewel was an event that occurred on the steps of the Fine Arts Building at Wellington. On bended knee I summoned the courage to ask you for your hand in marriage. It was easier asking you for your hand in marriage that afternoon than asking your father that morning out at your place in your barn as he milked Clara.

You have made my life far-reaching with none of the distractions and with the fewest of uncertainties. It has been bright, important, and meaningful. There is nothing I would alter except the time we have missed together because of this war. You were my first love; you were my last. Your touch, your warm embrace. That's what I cling to now. I thank you for being so extraordinarily special. You are my dream come true; a special treat in my life. You are the principal person in my life and I love you with all my heart... my total being. I have loved you always.

I can't count the times we sat there by my fireside in my backyard; the fire kept us warm as we watched the fireflies dance around the yard. Sitting quietly, holding hands, we'd look up at the stars and make wishes as one Flying Angel would suddenly shoot across the dark sky. I begged you to tell me your wish, but you always said it wouldn't come true if I knew the answer.

I regret that we never joined our names in marriage, but now I know the grief you would carry if we had. It is now an easier transition for you to go on without me. I want you to look forward to the future. Take a chance upon someone equal to or better than me.

My father always spoke about visions, predictions, or prophecies being fulfilled in a dream. Perhaps in the not too distant future you will have a dream and in the shadow of my life you will find someone else. Return to Wellington, and complete the life you've always wanted as a teacher. Reach young people as you have planned. Be their mentor. Carefully look for another Rose Ann and Eddie in the halls of CR. They're there somewhere. Help them find one another.

With All My Love,

Eddie

GLOSSARY OF TERMS
(ABBREVIATIONS USED)

A/C:	Aircraft
AD:	Academic Director
A/O:	Area of Operations
A4:	Single engine attack aircraft
Angels:	Reference to altitude. Ex: 5000 feet
As you were:	Informal command to continue what you were doing
Barracks:	Where single Marines live
Battalion:	Unit containing multiple military companies
Belay:	Stop
Betel Nut:	Narcotic seed nut chewed by VN villagers
Bingo:	Low fuel state, returning home base
Blowing smoke:	Wasting time; lying
BOQ:	Bachelor's Officers Quarters
Boot:	Recruit
Brain Fart:	Senior moment; moment of confusion
Brass:	Officers

Brig rat:	Always in trouble
Brown Bar:	Junior 2nd Lieutenant
Button 2:	Different frequency on radio
Bum scoop:	Bad information
Bush:	Outside the perimeter wire
Buy the Farm:	To be killed or to die
Call out:	Challenge to fight
Cat 9:	Beyond dumb
Cat 4:	Grades of being stupid
Charlie:	Communist soldier
Chicken Shit:	Petty
Chop Chop:	Hurry
Click:	Approximately one mile
Cluster Fuck:	Mission gone; bad confusion
COC:	Combat Operations Center
CO:	Commanding Officer
Company:	Unit containing more than one Platoon
CQ:	Carrier Qualifications
Deck:	Floor
DI:	Drill Instructor
DO:	Duty Officer
Dinged:	Wounded in Viet Nam
Dink:	Enemy soldier
Dinky Dau:	Crazy
Double time:	Run in step
DOW:	Died of wounds
DoZo:	Japanese for "please"

Duty:	Working at your post
E and E:	Escape and Evasion
ETA:	Estimated Time of Arrival
FAC:	Forward Air Controller; Assigned to ground units
FCLP:	Field carrier landing practice
Feather Merchant:	Little, small Marine
Feet Wet:	Going from land to over water during flight
Field of Fire:	Radius automatic can fire or cover from port to starboard
Flight Line:	Place where aircraft are parked
Flight surgeon:	Navy doctor assigned to Marine units
FMF:	Fleet Marine Force
FUBAR:	Fucked up beyond all recognition
Ground Pounder/Grunt:	Marine infantryman
HAC:	Helicopter Aircraft Commander
HAYAHU:	Japanese for "Hurry"
HMM:	Helicopter Medium Marine
HQ:	Headquarters
I Corps:	Most northern of four Corps areas into which Viet Nam was divided
JAG:	Judge Advocate General, Military Law Branch
Jelly:	Napalm
KIA:	Killed in Action
KP:	Kitchen duty

Lt.:	Lieutenant
LTJG:	Lt. Junior Grade US Navy
LZ:	Helicopter Landing Zone
MAG:	Marine Air Group
MAAG:	Marine Assistance Advisory Group
MARTD:	Marine Air Training Detachment
Maggot:	Lowest form of life
MarCad:	Marine aviation cadet
Mast:	Private meeting with Commanding Officer
May Day:	Distress signal
MCAS:	Marine Corps Air Station
MCRD:	Marine Corps Recruit Depot
Medivac:	Evacuation of wounded by helicopter
MIA:	Mission in Action
Milling around:	Wandering around, doing nothing
MOS:	Military Occupation Specialty
Muster:	Assemble
NABTC:	Naval Air Basic Training Command
NAS:	Naval Air Station
Newbie:	Newest member of a unit
NavCad:	Naval aviation cadet
NVA:	North Vietnamese Army
O Club:	Officers Only Club
OD:	Officer of the Day
OIC:	Officer in Charge
Passageway:	Hall

PCN:	Precision
PS:	Pre Solo
PFC:	Private First Class
Platoon:	Four Squads
Point:	Lead man on patrol
Quick time or QT:	120 steps a minute
RDO:	Runway Duty Officer
Regiment:	Four to six battalions
Rifling:	Illegal search
Roto Head:	Helicopter pilot
RPG:	Rocket-propelled grenade
S1:	Administration section of squadron
S2:	Intelligence Section
S3:	Operation Section
S4:	Logistics, supply, maintenance
Seabees:	Navy construction workers
Semper Fidelis:	Always faithful
Section:	Flight of two aircraft
Slack:	Ease off
SOP:	Standard operating procedures
SRB:	Service record book
Stand down:	Relieved of all duty
SSS:	Shit, shower and shave
Stow:	To put away
TACAN:	Navigation equipment
Tail End Charlie:	Last one in line
TAW:	Tactical Air Wing

TDY:	Temporary duty
VC:	Viet Cong
WIA:	Wounded in action
WUF:	Warm-up flight
085960:	Military ID Number
7335:	Military operational specialty number
0800H:	Time ("H" following the time means "hour")